LAZARUS HEART

LAZARUS HEART

MARY O'SULLIVAN

IGUANA

Publisher: Meghan Behse
Editor: Toby Keymer
Sculpture on front cover: "Reaching Out" by Dr. Michael Irving
Front cover photography: Lee Parpart

All quotes from Judith Lewis Herman are taken from *Trauma
and Recovery: The Aftermath of Violence - From Domestic
Abuse to Political Terror* by Judith L. Herman, copyright @
1992, 1997. Reprinted by permission of Basic Books, an imprint
of Hachette Book Group, Inc.

ISBN 978-1-77180-375-5 (paperback)
ISBN 978-1-77180-376-2 (epub)
ISBN 978-1-77180-377-9 (Kindle)

This is an original print edition of *Lazarus Heart*.

It is very tempting to take the side of the perpetrator. All the perpetrator asks is that the bystander do nothing. He appeals to the universal desire to see, hear, and speak no evil. The victim, on the contrary, asks the bystander to share the burden of pain.

—Judith Lewis Herman

TABLE OF CONTENTS

Introduction

When I started this book, my coach at the writers' program asked me why I was writing it. When I took it to an editor, I was asked who I was writing it for. And I imagine that you, the person reading this introduction, are wondering what you might come away with after reading this book. All good questions; all surprisingly hard to answer.

When "Chris" (not his real name, of course) came to live with me, we both found ourselves in a frightening and confusing situation as his memories began coming out. My strategy for understanding anything has always been to read up on it. The available books gave me a general idea about what post-traumatic stress disorder (PTSD) is and what causes it, but things like how to pull someone out of a full-on flashback, deal with nightmares, or treat eye-rolling with cough syrup were not in those books. Neither was the flesh and flavour of actually living day by day with an intractable mental illness, nor the life hacks that can help get you through the day. So, my first reason for writing this book was that this was the book I needed back then. And if you are someone living with complex PTSD, or you're the loved one or caregiver of someone in such a situation, I pray that this book will make things a little easier for you.

The second reason I wrote this book was that I found myself in a unique position to learn about PTSD. When the child psychologist Jean Piaget had children, he stayed home and took care of them from infancy on. His observations of his own children formed the basis of modern infant and child psychology. I found myself in a similar situation with regard to Chris. What are the odds that someone with a master's degree in applied psychology gets to study the full course of complex PTSD on a moment-by-moment basis for years? They say that the Chinese glyph for *crisis* includes the sign for *opportunity*; and I have to admit that I've had the opportunity to come up with some observations and questions that may spur further study. (For instance, the symptom of intractable vomiting doesn't respond well to anti-nausea medication. The real target may be the gag reflex.) One issue I would urge on professionals is to develop a protocol to differentially diagnose children with trauma from children with learning, attention, or intellectual challenges.

The third reason was that while there are (thank God) finally resources for female survivors of childhood abuse, the awareness of male childhood sexual abuse survivors is in its infancy. I swear it would have been faster and easier to just get Chris a sex change than to find him resources as a male abuse survivor. We need to fund social programs to support male victims. And, while they share many of the same symptoms of trauma with women, male survivors do have different issues around their experiences and may need different types of supports. For instance, Chris had handled his abuse by getting angry and fighting; a punching bag was a big part of his therapy.

Finally, I wrote this book because there are many Chrises out there, and with the influence of the Internet and the breakdown of social and community safety nets, there are going to be more. A lot more. In many ways, this is the story of a miracle. Like Lazarus, the real Chris was buried, while a numb, robotic version of him functioned in the real world. But finding him in there, and digging him out, was less like Christ's raising of Lazarus and more like pulling survivors out of a collapsed building. It took brutal amounts of time, energy, and resources for just one person. There are not enough miracles to go around. And in a society like ours, should a child have to depend on a miracle to survive?

Most children and teens like Chris end up homeless, on drugs, in jail, or dead from suicide. In Chris's case, and in the cases of so many children in our society, the systems that are supposed to offer protection either failed or colluded with the abusers. Parents, relatives, schools, hospitals, the police — in the end, even the agency I worked for — didn't protect or save Chris. Child sexual abuse is nothing less than slow motion murder, and it needs to be treated as such — by the police, by the schools, by the courts, by all levels of government. I wrote this book to get you to care about this, to get you involved, to get you *mad*! I hope, above all, that I accomplish this. If our children are not of value to us, what possibly can be?

Mary O'Sullivan

p.s. I was told that the layout of the book may be confusing to some readers. I'd like to explain the breakdown. There are three sections: I narrate the first and third sections, but the middle section is Chris's story, in his own words. I once read a remarkable book, *Annie's Coming Home* by

Rosemary Crossley. She describes how she brought a young, institutionalized woman home to live with her. Annie was nonverbal but able to communicate with an alphabet board. Part of the book is in Annie's words, and it was amazing to meet her within the story. I thought that the readers of this book should meet Chris, too.

PART I

MARY

Secrecy and silence are the perpetrator's first line of defense [...] If he cannot silence [the victim] absolutely, he tries to make sure that no one listens.

—Judith Lewis Herman

CHAPTER ONE

THE BOY IN THE WELL

I rang the bell and a big black Labrador answered the door. He shouldered his way through the opening, blundered against my legs, and snuffled a hearty, doggy welcome right into my groin. It was the most exuberant welcome I had ever received on a home visit.

"Back, Jack!" A short blond boy grabbed the dog's collar and pulled him back behind the door. "Sorry, he wasn't trying to hurt you. He's really friendly."

"Yes, I could tell that. Don't worry about it. I've got a husky at home."

While the boy was juggling the dog and the doorway to let me into the house, I introduced myself to him. "I guess your Aunt Olga told you that I'd be coming to meet you today, to help get things organized for your move."

"I'm Chris Logan. I'm pleased to meet you." He made momentary eye contact and shook my hand. This simple exchange was my first contact with the young man who would change my life in so many ways, and whose life I would end up saving.

I was a social worker for a non-profit agency at the time, coordinating services for people with developmental disabilities who lived with their families. Social work is a demanding job, especially in an underfunded area like Mississauga, Ontario. The scrounging I had to do to take care of some of my families took every ounce of my energy and brainpower. But I loved it. I carried about a hundred families on my caseload and I could rattle off the particulars of every client and their family, diagnoses, needs, resources, current issues, favourite foods, and tastes in music without looking at my notes. I ate disasters for breakfast and dunked crises in my coffee at break time. I was headed for a major burnout the following autumn, but in May 2001, I could still leap tall buildings in a single bound.

***

I was at my desk on a slow afternoon (at least what passed for slow in my job) when my phone rang. It was the mother of one of my clients asking for a favour. Could I call a friend of hers who needed some advice about social services? I didn't mind helping, especially since this client family had been really helpful with some of my projects, so I told her it would be no problem and contacted her friend, Olga Laszlo.

The next day, I met Olga at her home to discuss a rather unusual situation. We sat in her living room, which had that stiff, just-for-guests feeling, and I balanced my coffee cup on my notebook to avoid making rings on the furniture. Olga, fiftyish and firmly groomed, an administrator in a government agency, exchanged the obligatory pleasantries with me and got down to business.

"I need your advice, Mary, on a family situation. My nephew, my brother's son, is living in a boarding house in Kingston. His sister's been to see it and she says it's a terrible place. We're very worried about him. What I'd like to do is bring him here and get him into one of your agency's group homes. How could we arrange that?"

"Uh, well, Olga, something you should understand from the beginning is that we only serve individuals with intellectual disabilities. Does your nephew—"

"Oh, definitely, he's been in special education classes for years. He can't really take care of himself. His sister has been helping out, but she's in college and it's a real burden on her. He was living with a foster family and that was fine, but the place he's in now is just not safe."

"If you don't mind my asking, where are his parents?"

"His mother passed away several years ago. My brother lives here in Mississauga, but he's no help. To tell the truth, he's an alcoholic. The family's tried helping him, but that hasn't worked out at all." She picked up a photograph in a fancy gilded frame and passed it to me.

"That's my brother and his second wife with Janice and Chris." Her face tightened. "Chris didn't get along well with his stepmother. She wasn't a very nice woman."

I scanned the photo. A pretty standard grouping: a middle-aged man, stiff and thick-waisted in his suit, with a short, dark lady clutching his arm; the teenaged daughter in front of her father, smiling resolutely for the picture; and a slight boy, about thirteen, grimly looking off-camera and cringing away from the woman's hand on his shoulder.

I gave the photo back to Olga. "I think it's wonderful of you to be helping out this way. I'm wondering … If Chris had a foster family, he's probably already involved with services in that area. If I were you, I'd start with them for a residential placement, because we have very long waiting lists for group home spots in this region. Chris couldn't even begin to apply for services unless he was living here."

"Well, we really want him here where the family can take care of him. Is there any way we can start applying for services now, and then we can move him?"

"Olga, I'd like to help you out, but unless he lives here, there isn't much I can do. But I really respect your doing all this for your nephew. If you can get him here, I wouldn't mind lending a hand unofficially until he has some services set up."

"Well, I appreciate that very much. Carla said you were a very helpful person. Could I get your number in case I have any other questions? You seem to know so much about this business, and it's all new to me."

I gave her my card, shook hands with her, and left. I didn't spend much time thinking about it, although I was a bit curious about whether they would have any luck with the Kingston agencies. I did feel that Olga was applying a bit of pressure, which I had dealt with before and wasn't bothered by. I come across as a frowzy, middle-aged social worker type, glasses and all: very non-threatening. Most of the time it helps people open up, but for some it's a sign of weakness. I've had to learn to set boundaries when necessary.

A month later, I heard back from Olga. She had moved her nephew in with her family and wanted my help with setting up services for him in Mississauga. I had to admit, I was impressed with her commitment, so I agreed to meet Chris and do some intake paperwork.

A week later, I was back at the Laszlo home shaking hands with Chris. I knew he was twenty-one, but he could have fit in on any high school campus as a sophomore. It wasn't just his small build or his baby face; he seemed physically young for his age. He was clean-shaven, short-haired, and dressed in Dockers and a polo shirt. My social worker brain registered excellent social skills and verbal ability, but his body language suggested a natural shyness overlaid with a patina of maturity.

I had almost made it inside by now. Jack had caught the husky scent and was sniffing hopefully at my briefcase.

"Would you like to sit in the living room?" Chris asked.

"Well, we have a lot of paperwork to do and it's easier to write at a table."

"We could sit in the kitchen if you want. I can put Jack in the basement if he's bothering you." Jack was already halfway to the kitchen, waiting on us and wagging his tail expectantly. I hated to hurt his feelings by having him shut up. I also had a sense that Chris would feel more comfortable with his dog there. An intake interview can be a long and intrusive process. Most of the time, parents or other family members completed the intakes, since my agency served people with intellectual disabilities who often couldn't answer or even understand the questions. But Chris seemed ready to handle the situation on his own.

Chris led me to an unpretentious kitchen with a small dinette set pushed into the corner. It had a more relaxed vibe than the living room. I spread out my paperwork on the table while Jack found a comfortable position underneath. Chris politely offered me a Coke. I accepted, as I always do on home visits, because it puts the other person in the role of host and creates a bond at the start of the interview. I noticed that Chris didn't get a drink for himself but sat down across from me and waited.

First, I needed him to sign some forms, so I gave my standard speech, simplified a bit so he could understand it. I was careful to point out the signature lines in case he didn't read. Chris signed in a large, round, scrawling cursive hand at what looked to be about a seven- or eight-year-old level. I noticed large calluses on his hands as he was writing, on the lower parts of both thumbs and inside the knuckles of his forefingers. He saw me looking and moved his hands beneath the table. "I have a skin problem. I'm putting lotion on it." I pretended I hadn't noticed and went on with the interview.

"I understand that you're going to be moving here from Kingston at the beginning of September."

"Yes, I'm going to be living here with my Aunt Olga and Uncle Ian and my cousins. My Aunt Olga even got me in a college program. I'm starting on September 12."

There was a glimmer of excitement behind his expression, and it suddenly struck me that it was a poker face — that his politeness had a wariness about it. Chris wasn't the only one at the table going through an intake process: he was evaluating me as thoroughly as I was evaluating him.

"Your aunt said you're living in a sort of a boarding house."

"Well, yeah, there's six of us living there," he told me. He seemed to focus on the forms in front of him as if he could visualize the information on them, but his tone of voice was quite casual, as if he were talking about school activities. "We each have our own room. The rooms are really small. I just have my bed and my TV with my Nintendo system, and a cupboard for my clothes. We share the bathroom and the kitchen and the living room, and the phone and everything. The landlady does the meals and the cleaning.

"It's not a bad place, but all the other men living there are a lot older than me. They aren't dangerous or anything, but one of the guys is schizophrenic, I think, and he keeps telling me that I'm messing with his mind. It's going to be better living here with my aunt and uncle."

"Before the boarding house, you were living with a foster family?" If another agency had accessed funding for Chris, I needed to see about the possibility of transferring it.

Chris seemed to tighten up at this question. "When I was living with my dad, Dan and Denise lived in the next apartment. Dad moved back to Toronto and I didn't have any place to stay, so I moved in with them."

"Did they get money from the government for taking care of you? Did you have someone like me who would come to the house and check on you?"

"Not really. I got money from the government but Denise had my bank card. When I graduated and I was working at Wendy's, she would cash my paycheque and give me an allowance. I think she got money from my family too. She would get me to write letters and ask them."

"Did you like living with Dan and Denise?"

His face became animated for the first time. "I hated it there, but there wasn't anywhere else to go. I was so glad when I moved into that boarding house and had my own place."

Then he shrugged and fiddled with the papers in front of him. "My sister Janice visited me, and then Aunt Olga told me to move out here with her until I could find a place near them."

I was getting the picture. No agencies involved. This father just took off and left his kids twisting in the wind. So why were the relatives getting involved now? That boarding house must have been a serious hellhole to scare them into action.

We got the last of the forms filled out and signed. Chris stood politely and waited as I packed up the mess of paperwork. Jack had apparently found the intake process boring and there was a deep vibrato snore coming from under the table. As Chris walked me to the door, it occurred to me that he hadn't asked anything. I pulled out one of my business cards for him.

"If you have any questions or need any help with the move, feel free to give me a call." This was a pretty standard comment on ending an interview.

He took my card carefully and examined it, then pulled a thick wallet out of his back pocket and filed it meticulously into a large collection of cards, photos, and notes.

I walked back to my car imagining the sniffing-over I would be getting from my husky that evening: "You slut, you've been out with another dog!" A jealous spouse is nothing next to a possessive pet.

On the drive back to the office, I kept going over the interview in my mind. Overall, Chris presented as having a bona fide disability. He had the all-important IQ score of 80, which put him in the "borderline" range of intellectual disability and qualified him for government services. But his being identified as intellectually disabled in his teens was strange. Except for cases of brain damage, most clients are identified as "special needs" by early grade school at the latest. His move from North Bay, which may not have had a policy of labelling students, to the Ottawa school district may have accounted for that. Still, Chris had poor handwriting, no money skills, and difficulty organizing information. He would have had a hard time living on his own.

I had a master's degree in psychology and twelve years' experience working with intellectually disabled clients. Chris had check marks by all the right items, but, having been trained in intellectual assessment, I also knew where it could go wrong. Learning disabilities or psychological problems can skew the results of IQ tests. Having read between the lines of the school report Chris's aunt had provided me, I had gotten the feeling that the psychometrist who wrote it had gotten some disturbing vibes about the situation. After meeting Chris, so had I. I just wasn't sure why.

There was the possibility of an autistic disorder such as Asperger's syndrome. Chris was obviously well trained in polite behaviour, but he had shown very little emotion during the interview — he had become a bit excited about the move to Mississauga and upset momentarily once or twice, but that was all. He was passive and uninvolved, like someone playing a part. As my mind reviewed autism symptoms, it suddenly hit me. The calluses I had noticed were familiar; I had seen them on several autistic clients who self-stimulated by chewing on their hands.

But an autistic person wouldn't have been self-conscious about his hands, and Chris had made up an excuse for them. For another thing, he'd glanced at me sideways. In my experience, someone who was autistic either looked at something or didn't. Their head would move in the same direction as their eyes. There were other subtleties in his voice and movements that should not have been there in someone with either Asperger's or an intellectual disability.

And he laughed at my jokes! Smiled briefly, anyway, at the right moments. While I wouldn't go so far as to say that appreciating my humour is a sign of intelligence, there is a correlation between intelligence and the type of humour a person understands. I tend to have a dry sense of humour; it's surprisingly handy with nonverbal clients. One girl who was quadriplegic and unable to respond verbally cracked up when I made a pun. That requires abstract reasoning. Intellectually disabled clients usually look confused or ignore my jokes, and autistic people look at me like I'm crazy. While Chris wasn't exactly the life of the party, there was a sense of humour in there somewhere.

Actually, that was my whole impression of Chris. There were a lot of things "in there somewhere." Somehow, those things were disconnected from his day-to-day functioning; hence, the diagnosis of intellectual disability. Most likely there was some combination of learning disability and psychological disorder going on. But, if something looks like a duck and quacks like a duck, any bureaucracy will call it a duck. And Fate had put this odd duck on my caseload.

As I focused on finding a parking space, one final impression stayed with me. It was something in Chris's eyes. I remembered an odd bit of science trivia about wells: the depth and narrowness of a well shaft blocks out ambient sunlight so you can look up in the daytime and see only black sky. In fact, there are telescopes designed on this principle — they produce a perpetual view of the stars by being deep enough to create an artificial night. That was the look in Chris's eyes: the look of someone gazing up from the bottom of a very deep well.

Chapter Two

Breaking the Surface

Chris had been on my caseload for eight months and, of the hundred-odd clients assigned to me, he was one of the lowest priority cases — he had a place to stay, a program to go to, and he was able to use the bus by himself. I had helped connect him to some resources, got his disability benefits transferred to Peel Region, and sent in an application for housing that, with luck, would come through before he was eligible for an old-age home.

While Chris was low on my list of worries, there were some issues with his aunt. When he had first moved in with her family, she was a model of competence and was ready to do anything to help her nephew. But after a few months, the reality of that responsibility started to settle in on her, and the smooth veneer of concern was stripping off to reveal the warped wood underneath. At least once a week, Aunt Olga was on the phone to me with another complaint about Chris. He drank (one beer). He smoked. He used drugs (aspirin). He was skipping school (on reading week). Finally, she demanded a group home placement for Chris, or she was going to send him back to the boarding house in Kingston. One of the home support workers confided in me that Chris seemed terrified of his aunt. Not that

Chris would have been hard to terrify, but by then I had seen enough of Aunt Olga's bad side to sympathize with him.

It wasn't a joke that people in Peel could (and often did) die of old age waiting for the kind of group home placement Aunt Olga was demanding. Most people with intellectual disabilities lived with their families. But Chris didn't have any other family to live with, so I was going to have to come up with something — and soon.

In May, we caught two strokes of luck. First, Chris's pre-vocational course at the local community college included a work placement. Chris was the top of his class and his teacher was really impressed with his willingness to work. When Chris couldn't find a placement, the teacher helped set him up with one. The supervisor was also impressed. Chris's placement turned into a full-time job that paid enough for him to have a place of his own.

Then my friend Barbara and her husband agreed to rent Chris a basement apartment in their new home, a big, brick, two-storey dwelling that backed onto a greenbelt, where they saw deer from their bedroom windows in the mornings. I had known Barbara for ten years. When we met, she was a single mother with a disabled daughter, Annie, struggling to pay rent on a two-bedroom apartment. This was her dream house and it felt good to see her and Annie there with Barbara's new husband, Arthur. We arranged for a home visit to see the place and introduce Chris.

I brought Chris over after supper. Barbara had been baking. The kitchen smelled wonderful, and Barbara offered Chris some cookies. Arthur introduced himself affably before going off to work. The rest of us sat around the kitchen table. Barb's daughter came in to check out the new guy — and for the cookies. Annie was like a big cuddly puppy in human form. She loved practically everyone, and Chris seemed to really enjoy the attention from her. He warmed to Barbara as well; she was very reassuring about the living arrangements, and I explained anything I felt he didn't understand.

The basement was set up with its own bathroom and kitchen, and it was clean and spacious. Chris's bedroom was a big, homey family room, already furnished, with a fireplace, a big-screen TV, and living room furniture that Barbara had left for him. He had his own entrance through the garage and a lock on his door. He walked around like the master of his domain, laying out his new life in his mind as he planned out his bachelor pad with his bed in the corner.

I was mentally checking Chris off as an active issue on my casefile. Job placement — done. Residential placement — done. I was doing a little victory dance in my head.

Looking back, I think I was being a bit naive.

If you blow up a balloon underwater, you can give yourself an insane headache. I'm not recommending it — the point is that while the balloon is under water, it can hold in a lot of air pressure because the water pressure outside the balloon equalizes it. But if you take the balloon out of the water and into the air, the outside pressure lessens and the balloon expands, and usually explodes. People who have a lot of pressure inside are the same: difficulties in their lives can distract from and "hold down" inner issues. Until, of course, their lives improve.

I could almost see Chris's personality expanding as he moved into his new apartment. Although I didn't know it at the time, what I was seeing was a balloon breaking the surface.

Once Chris moved in, I became a lot more involved. Barbara and I had been friends for years, and she was doing this partly as a favour for me. I wanted to make sure everything went well. Besides, I was getting fond of Chris. He was very sweet-natured, and he tried so hard at everything.

But there was more to it than that. Mother Teresa once said, "find your own Calcutta." Every person has to find the place in their life where God wants them to be in order to do the tasks God has planned for them to do. As a deeply religious person who had become deeply disillusioned with religion, I practised my faith through my work. And every now and then, I felt as if God were whispering in the back of my mind that I was doing one for Him. More and more, I was getting that feeling about Chris.

From May to June, Chris couldn't have been happier. He had a job at a woodworking factory helping with cleanup, deliveries, and odd jobs. Sometimes he even did sanding and assembly. His coworkers were good to him and his boss was very supportive. He worked five full days a week and half-days on Saturdays, and, even with the hour-long commute by bus twice a day, Chris had a perfect attendance record. He loved having a job.

As I got to know him better, I discovered that he was very shy about having anyone do him a favour. If I bought him lunch at McDonald's, he would spend the entire meal thanking me and promising to pay me back. He apologized for everything and would usually throw in an extra "I'm sorry" every few minutes in case he'd missed one.

And he never smiled. He could produce a tight-lipped grimace if a situation required it, but never a real smile. He reminded me of Eeyore, the donkey in the *Winnie the Pooh* books. This really showed itself when I invited him to a music festival with my youth group. He spent the day wandering glumly behind the others until I got worried and asked if he was okay.

Chris seemed genuinely surprised. "I'm having a great time. Thanks for inviting me." And off he went, looking just as morose as before.

He also never talked about his past. He could talk about every detail of his day at work, but his past seemed to have been erased. If I asked about his mother, who had died of lung cancer when Chris was eleven, he would say, "I loved my mom. She smoked a lot, but she was a really good mother."

"Do you remember anything else about her?"

"No, not really."

In those early days, the only time he mentioned his past was to tell me a story about a vacation his family had taken when he was fourteen. They had visited his stepmother's family in Honduras for the summer. After one of the appointments I had taken him to, while we were walking back to the car, Chris just brought it up casually in the conversation.

"My back teeth were coming in and my mouth wouldn't close all the way. The dentist said that they would have to be pulled. So while we were in Honduras, my stepmother Ursula decided to take me to the dentist down there. It was really old-style. The chair was old-looking, with red leather cushions on it and it had a high back like an old barber's chair.

"The dentist picked up a long-handled thing with a clamp on the end and a small hammer, about this big. Then he tells me to open my mouth and he sticks the clamp in my mouth. I'm going, 'Wait a minute, aren't you forgetting something? Aren't you gonna freeze it?' And he says 'No, we don't use that down here. Hold still, I do this real fast.'

"Then he gets the clamp around the tooth and he's going *yank, yank* and *tap, tap* with the hammer," (Chris pantomimed the action), "but the tooth won't come out. I'm swearing like crazy because it hurts so much but he has the clamp in my mouth so it comes out like 'hold on, thtop, thuck oo, thuck oo, sssit!' I'm holding onto the armrests of the chair, they're made of brass, real solid, and I'm bending them because I'm pulling so hard. He was kind of upset about that after but, I mean, what did he expect?

"He's having a hard time getting the tooth out, so he starts wiggling it sideways. I guess he's getting mad because he keeps saying, 'Puta! Puta!' I think that means 'bitch' in Spanish. He got all four teeth out but this one broke in half," he pointed to his right upper jaw, "and he had to take it out in two pieces. I couldn't swear anymore because my mouth was swollen up and it hurt too much. When I looked in the mirror, my teeth looked all bloody. It was really gross."

I was speechless. And this seemed to worry Chris. He was watching me closely out of the corner of his eye, waiting for my response as if something important depended on it. I wasn't sure what response to make. The story was too awful to believe but I had learned long ago that reality isn't confined to what we want to believe. I had to choose. Either it wasn't true, and I was supposed to call him on it, or it was true, and I was supposed to show I believed him.

"Where was your stepmother when all this was happening?"

"Ursula was on a stool next to me. She was watching the whole thing with this creepy smile on her face."

"God, I just can't believe this!" The words slipped out before I could stop them.

"No, it's the truth! I'm not making this up!" He spun to face me, horrified, and I realized that I had said the absolute wrong thing.

"No, no, I believe you. I just can't imagine someone ... doing that."

He relaxed and nodded, pacified. "Yeah, she was a bitch. I hated her."

I wasn't as sure about believing him as I sounded. It was beyond doubt the strangest thing I'd ever been told, and I had been a social worker for years. On the one hand, I didn't sense that Chris was making it up. I've talked to compulsive liars and they tend to get grandiose as they go along, looking for a reaction in their listeners. Chris wasn't trying to impress me. He was more concerned about being believed. He also came up with details that you wouldn't think of. It was as if he were running a video of the experience in his head and describing it to me rather than simply remembering it.

On the other hand, he had told the whole story in a conversational tone, as if he were describing a trip to the grocery store. In the end, though, there was a little anger seeping out when he called his stepmother a bitch. That was the most emotion I had ever seen in Chris, although it was still pretty mild considering what he had been through.

And that was the strangest part. How does a fourteen-year-old boy sit still in a chair while someone pulls out his teeth without anaesthetic? I couldn't have held still like that at gunpoint. And why would he do it simply because his stepmother told him to? Most parents can't get their teenagers to clean up their rooms. And she had watched. It gave me a cold feeling up my backbone to think about it. If this was a standard example of what his life had been like, there were some very disturbing things floating around in that locked-up brain.

We talked about trivial things on the way home and he actually seemed cheerful when I dropped him off. I had the distinct feeling that I had passed some kind of test.

CHAPTER THREE

THE TIES THAT BIND — AND GAG

Even though he was on his own, I still expected Chris to get some support from his family, but I didn't know until later that Aunt Olga was constantly making phone calls and writing letters to Barbara telling her how to manage Chris's life. Chris hated being talked about behind his back and treated like a child, but at that point he still couldn't speak up about it.

Worst of all, Olga got Chris's father back into his life. This surprised me, since Olga knew that her brother Edvard had been a terrible father to Chris. Even after dumping Chris with the neighbours back in Ottawa four years earlier, Eddie hadn't benefited from the alcohol rehab program. He had stayed with Olga's family for a year or so until she kicked him out. Since then, he had been living in boarding houses and basement apartments, finding part-time jobs to supplement his senior's pension.

The first time I met Eddie was at Chris's apartment. He was wearing a polyester leisure suit that had seen better days, as had the body inside it. He was portly and had the "gin blossom" nose of a chronic alcoholic. He looked like a creepy

W. C. Fields. Still, I found him articulate, a little self-important, but fairly convincing as the prodigal parent.

As I introduced myself, Eddie shook my hand with a professional warmth as if we were colleagues. He then said that he wanted to talk to me without Chris present. This wasn't unusual with other client families, but I had an eerie feeling about it, so I explained that it was against agency policy to exclude the client from meetings. Eddie was somewhat disgruntled but accepted my decision. He went on to express concern for his son's situation and show interest in being involved in Chris's life. And then, while Chris sat there, Eddie explained to me that his son was not capable of living on his own, that he was unreliable and irresponsible and tended to exaggerate, "heh, heh." I had reason to remember that conspiratorial chuckle later on.

It occurred to me that Eddie was speaking with a lot of authority about someone he hadn't seen for four years. I pointed that out, politely, and also told him that everyone who had dealt with Chris, both at his college program and his new job, was very impressed with him.

Eddie visibly deflated, like a blowfish shrinking down to a flat blob. Obviously, I was supposed to be agreeing with him and I wasn't getting with the program. Chris sat there like the Sphinx, but inside he was doing the whole production of Riverdance singlehandedly. Apparently, I had been the first person in his experience to shut Eddie down. The interview ended rather abruptly after that.

After meeting Eddie, I thought nothing had been accomplished. I couldn't have been more wrong. Chris's family had very little to do with me directly. I might even say they avoided me. Most of the time, Olga spoke to Barbara if there was anything she needed to discuss about Chris. This was fine, since the family was usually the client's primary support system, and I thought nothing of it. I didn't find out until later that both Eddie and Olga were telling Barbara that Chris was irresponsible and untrustworthy. Chris knew what was going on and he was very frustrated by it. He remembered how his family had colluded with Dan and Denise, the foster family he'd lived with years ago, to keep him under control, and he could see it happening all over again. But he was also afraid to say anything to anyone, even me. He knew how persuasive his family could be, and he still wasn't sure what to expect from me.

I found out much later that Eddie was also coming by almost every day, saying hi to Chris but then hanging out upstairs with Barbara and her family. A couple of times, the family came home and found him camped out in the backyard waiting for them. Other times, Chris would see Eddie parked in his car up the street, just watching the house for hours.

And Barbara was starting to complain about Chris — little things that wouldn't normally have bothered her: Chris not cleaning his bathroom properly or going out for hamburgers instead of eating meals with the family. When I asked her if she wanted any help dealing with it, she shrugged and said it wasn't important.

While his family seemed to be shutting me out, Chris opened up to me remarkably — or remarkably for him. We actually started to have conversations about at least one part of his past: the four years he had spent with Dan and Denise.

After Eddie had left Ursula, Chris and his sister stayed with her. When Chris was sixteen, Ursula made him move in with his father. They had shared an apartment for a year or two; Eddie was drinking heavily at the time and Chris was more or less fending for himself. He had become friends with the people in the apartment next door. They had a son his age and the mother was nice to him when he came over. At some point, Eddie packed up and left for an alcoholism rehab program in Mississauga without making any arrangements for Chris. The neighbours invited him to move in with them and he did.

I already knew something about Dan and Denise. Olga told me that collection companies had been phoning about credit card debts — apparently, the foster parents had made Chris apply for credit cards, then took them and ran up large debts on them. I contacted the collection agencies and provided them with letters explaining that Chris had a disability and had not used the credit cards. Paper with an agency letterhead works wonders sometimes; the collection calls stopped. That was the last I heard of Dan and Denise for almost a year.

After the interview with Eddie, Chris started talking about Dan and Denise again. And talking. And talking. And getting madder and madder. It was like a crack in a dam, a deluge of anger coming out from behind that frozen persona Chris wore. Once he started talking about them, he couldn't stop.

And it wasn't just anger. It was outrage. And there was plenty to be outraged about. I heard about it every time I took Chris out for appointments or lunch.

"At first I was really happy to be there. I even called Denise 'Mom' for a while. Then she started getting mad at me for little things. I didn't know what was happening, I just started thinking, 'Oh no, not again!' I thought it was going to be like it was with my stepmother. Denise got mad at everybody, she even yelled at Dan. She fought with her son Mark a lot because he yelled back, but Melvin was her favourite. He was the youngest and he had a learning disability or something. He wasn't great at school and he didn't have friends because he was fucking obnoxious. I got along with Mark until he moved out, but Melvin was always calling me a retard.

"I was in a special class because I was having a really hard time concentrating. Denise was always telling me I was like my dad, that I had bipolar disorder or something, that I had the mind of a five-year-old. She treated me like a child. I couldn't go out after dark or over to friends' houses. She would get mad because I ate too slow. So I'd eat faster and then she'd get mad because I was stuffing my face. I got so freaking nervous all the time, because whatever I did, I was going to get shit for it. When I went to bed, I would cry for hours. I didn't make any noise because I was afraid she'd hear me.

"Denise was in a wheelchair so there was stuff she couldn't do, but she never got Melvin or Dan to do anything. She'd get me up at eight o'clock on Saturday mornings to start vacuuming the living room. I'd come home after a twelve-hour shift and there would be a sink full of dishes waiting for me. And she'd take my paycheque and give me ten dollars for cigarette money. I'd be working sixty hours a week sometimes and I never had any money.

"That was when I started to apologize all the time. Whenever Denise started to look upset, I'd say, 'Did I do something, Denise? I'm sorry, I'm sorry.' She would accuse me of stuff all the time and, even if I didn't do it, I would confess just to shut her up."

Chris would get louder and angrier as he talked until, sometimes, I had to ask him to quiet down. This was such a contrast to his usual locked-down behaviour that I started to worry. I decided to hook Chris up with mental health resources, and in late June I got him an intake appointment at the Community Mental Health Clinic. We met with Dr. Vindar, the staff psychiatrist, and she felt that Chris might benefit from an anger management program starting in the fall. Getting any psychological help for people with intellectual disabilities, which was Chris's diagnosis at that time, was next to impossible, so I was fairly encouraged. I also took Dr. Vindar's card for Chris's file, which turned out to be a lifesaver three months later.

As I listened to Chris venting about Denise, I noticed the same pattern to his memories. He had almost a photographic memory for details and made a point of recounting the first and last names of neighbours, street names and apartment numbers. Again, he seemed to be watching a videotape in his head and describing it to me. On the other hand, he was at a loss as to what age he was when these things happened and would be off by years from one guess to the next.

After getting to know what his family was like, I wasn't as shocked as I should have been that Chris had been left with Dan and Denise for four years. Still, I had to ask if he'd told his family what was going on.

"They wouldn't have listened to me. Denise kept in touch with my family; Janice came by every month, and they'd sit down together and discuss me like I was a child. And if I complained, or if I didn't do everything Denise said, she threatened to phone Eddie on me. I hated it, but I didn't have anywhere else to go."

"Did you ever think of asking to move out here? I mean, your aunt let you stay with her for a while."

"They wouldn't have let me smoke and Denise did. I was smoking like a madman back then. It was the only thing that calmed my nerves."

"Once you were an adult, you didn't have to ask, you know. You had a job. You could have just left."

"I didn't know how. A couple of times I tried, like when Mark moved out, I was going to stay with him, or my manager at Wendy's offered to let me move in with him. But Denise would tell everyone that I was handicapped and I would be too big a responsibility. A lady from social services was getting me a place with two other men my age and Denise pretended to agree to it. Then she moved to Kingston and took me with her."

"Well, you've got your own place now, at Barbara's. Your own job and your own money. I bet Denise would have a fit if she could see you now. You really showed her, didn't you?"

"Yeah," Chris mused, a little smile playing on his face. "Yeah, I guess I did."

Chapter Four

The Balloon Pops

It was August and Chris had been at his job for four months when his supervisor phoned me to tell me Chris had had a heart attack.

I was shocked to get the call since Chris seemed really healthy. He'd been complaining of being tired for the past month or so, but he worked long hours at the factory. I phoned the emergency room and was relieved to hear that Chris had been sent home. His "heart attack" had turned out to be an anxiety attack.

The next day, I took Chris back to Dr. Vindar. She diagnosed Chris with an anxiety disorder, gave him some prescriptions, and told him to stay home from work for six weeks or so to give the medication time to take effect. We didn't know it then, but Chris would not work again for fifteen years.

On the ride home from the doctor, Chris told me that he had visited his mom's family in Sudbury in July. It was a good visit, but when he got back, he started feeling sad all the time and crying when there wasn't anything the matter. I asked him if he'd had anxiety attacks like this one before.

"Not this bad. But I've been having trouble breathing lately. I thought my asthma was acting up. I'm not sleeping much, and it's been hard to get up in the morning and sometimes I miss my bus. But the buses were just running slow this morning and I couldn't do anything about it. I started getting nervous on the bus, people were looking at me, but I couldn't calm down. When I got to work, I was crying.

"I think I scared Jim a little. I just kept apologizing. He told me to go in the coffee room and relax and start in when I was ready. I thought I was calmed down and I got my coveralls on. But when I went to my station, I couldn't breathe and my chest hurt like crazy. Then the ambulance guys came and took me to the hospital. I still have my coveralls at home. I have to get them back to Jim."

Damn! Just when everything was going so well for him. But I had handled worse situations than this. I had to make sure Chris didn't lose his job or his apartment while he recovered. That meant a meeting with his boss, who was sympathetic and willing to hold his job for him, an application for short-term disability pension, and a conference with his Aunt Olga, who felt that the best thing for Chris was to get right back to work. I renegotiated his rent, got his prescriptions filled and took him to psychiatric appointments. A few weeks of crisis management would be well worth it if Chris could just hang on to the life he had worked so hard to put together.

But Chris wasn't getting better. Six weeks came and went and there was no way he could return to work. He couldn't concentrate. His asthma came back with a vengeance. He had insomnia and nightmares. He began stammering again, which he hadn't done since junior high school. He became terrified of being alone downstairs in his apartment and he developed the weirdest tic I had ever seen: he would suddenly gasp and flinch, looking over his shoulder as if something were behind him. He would do this three or four times in a row before he could stop himself. The tic would repeat every few minutes. I was afraid he would give himself whiplash.

Worst of all, Chris was humiliated. He had no idea why all this was happening and just wanted it to stop. He wanted to go back to work and be normal. And his family continued to pressure him about returning to work, even after I repeatedly explained that his supervisor could not let him back without a doctor's consent. I had seen many reactions to illness or disability, but I had never seen anything like this. The sicker Chris got, the more obsessive his family became about him working. That seemed to be the only thing they worried about, and from where I stood, it was the least of his worries.

When the short-term disability funding started running out, I helped reactivate Chris's case with long-term funding, but that wasn't going to cover his rent, so I also started an application for emergency residential funding. Even that was going to take months, but I hoped he would hang on until then.

One afternoon in late September, my supervisor and I did a home visit with Chris to complete the funding application. Chris asked me to stay after. We sat in his TV area. Chris was trembling, hunched up on the sofa across from where I sat, cross-legged on the easy chair (my thinking position).

"I had a nightmare," he said. "It was so real. I was sitting right where you are, and I heard a knock — quiet, like a scratching almost. There was a draught under the door and some dead leaves blew in. And there was a smell like wet, rotting earth. Somebody was mumbling something, but I couldn't hear what it was. And I was too scared to open the door. I couldn't move. Then the handle turned and the door opened really slow.

"It was my mom. I mean, it was her corpse, all rotted and flesh falling off. Her collarbone and some of her ribs on the right side were bare white bone. She only had one eye and the other was an empty black socket. Something moved in there and then a mouse came out of her eyehole and dropped on the floor and ran under the couch. Her clothes were torn up and rotted and you could see through them to her body. Pieces of skin were falling off and there were maggots underneath wriggling around. The smell was putrid." Chris was breathing heavily now, his shoulders clenched and his eyes fixed on the doorway.

"She came inside, slow, because she was pulling something. One of the bones on her forearm, the lower bone" — he pointed to his own arm — "fell off and she had to stop to pick it up and put it back. She was pulling a coffin. She lifted it up like it didn't weigh anything and put it on the coffee table, right here. It was closed but it had dirt on it like it had just been dug up. She was standing over the coffin and mumbling something, but she couldn't say it because her tongue was all dried up. Then she sat down on the sofa, right next to me. I still couldn't move; I wanted to, but my body wouldn't. She put her arm around me. I could feel how dry the skin was and the smell got worse. Then she put her face really close, like she was trying to kiss me. That's when I woke up."

We were both silent for a moment. Chris was slumped over, drained, and I was feeling queasy. I wasn't sure what to say, and then my psychology background kicked in and I remembered something about dream interpretation from a therapy class I had taken.

"This might be what's been causing your anxiety. I mean, you were only eleven when your mom died. You have a hard time even remembering her and maybe that's because you buried the whole experience. Do you remember if you went to her funeral?"

He blinked a few times, as if mentally changing gears. "Yeah, I remember going with my aunt and uncle, and my sister. I saw the casket at the front of the church. It was reddish-brown wood, almost like that colour." He pointed at the entertainment unit. "But a bit darker and polished. It had brass handles. The top was closed. I went up to the casket, and I remember that I knocked on it three times. That's when it hit me that my mother was inside it and she was really dead. I hadn't cried until then, but I ran to my aunt and buried my face in her coat and just howled."

I couldn't help but notice that Chris related this memory in his dispassionate, how-I-spent-my-summer-vacation voice. It struck me that when he had described the nightmare, he had spoken with really strong emotion.

"It must have been terrifying to think of her in the casket," I continued. "So maybe your mother in the dream is how you felt about her being dead. Kids can imagine some grisly stuff. And the emotions you felt in the dream were things you couldn't feel back then. Now you're strong enough to deal with them, so your subconscious is letting them out."

He looked somewhat reassured, so I went on. "You've been through a lot and that probably means that a lot of stuff got piled up in the back of your mind because you weren't able to deal with it at the time. So what we have to do is start shovelling it out so that you have enough space in there to deal with getting back to work."

Chris seemed positively cheerful at the idea until I said, "I have to get back to the office now. Are you going to be okay?"

"Sure, I'm fine," he said, now with a totally panicked look on his face.

"Is Barbara home yet? Is there anybody upstairs? I don't think you should be by yourself right now."

"I'll be okay."

"Chris, you look white as a ghost. Would you like to hang out with Dana at my place till tonight?" Dana was a young woman who rented my basement, and Chris had met her a few times. She was from Newfoundland and was really funny and down to earth.

Chris hesitated, then smiled shyly. "Well, if it's okay with you and Dana."

I went out into the hall to phone home and Chris followed me — closely. He didn't actually touch me, but you couldn't have gotten a sheet of paper between us. As we left, he went through that darkened hallway to the outside door like Jack the Ripper was hiding in the shadows, and on the drive back to my house his tic was so bad I was afraid he'd strangle himself on the seat belt's shoulder strap.

Chris spent the afternoon watching TV and chatting with Dana and her boyfriend, and by the time I arrived to drive him home he was smiling and chatting, looking completely relaxed. But on the drive back to Barbara's place, his tic started again. I had a sense that things were starting to unravel.

Over the next three months, Zombie Mom, as we named the nightmare figure, kept showing up in Chris's dreams. The creepy part was that she started trying to hug and kiss him, and in one dream she actually shoved him back on the bed and crawled on top of him. Chris was terrified of her but couldn't fight back. His body would just freeze.

I had some thoughts about what was going on, but this time I didn't say anything. From my viewpoint, Ursula the stepmother was a better candidate for the Zombie Mom than

Chris's real mother. And if the dreams were any indication, she did more to this kid than get his teeth yanked. Chris wasn't catching on to this, though, and he still had no real memories of his childhood or teens. I had read some books on sexual abuse and knew that repression, the mind's trick of sucking down traumatic memories into the quicksand of the subconscious, was a common way to deal with experiences of abuse. But to repress your whole life?

CHAPTER FIVE

...THEN IT FALLS APART

Things began going downhill faster at Chris's place. Soon, he was staying up all night, going to the garage and smoking. He would open the automatic door to let the smoke out, which often woke Barbara and Arthur. And I suspected that Barbara thought he was on drugs because of his constant nervousness and poor concentration. Chris began feeling insecure with Barbara and Arthur and started avoiding them. He was also having trouble managing his money and came up short on the rent.

Then Barbara told me that she thought Chris was taking money out of her purse at night. The peculiar thing was that Barbara was very experienced with children who had behavioural problems and normally would have been able to deal with issues like this. But something about Chris was triggering an unusual hostility in her. I knew that she had come from a difficult family background and the only explanation I could come up with was that Chris was stirring up old memories for her. I think her feelings toward him confused even her. She would rant on about him, but when I asked if I should work on getting him somewhere else to live, she would tell me not to worry about it.

The crisis came in early October. Chris had gone with Barbara and her family to visit her relatives in Newfoundland for a week. When they returned, he was a nervous wreck. The neck tic was back with a vengeance. I took him out to lunch at Wendy's to try to find out what was wrong. He told me that Barbara had accused him of stealing two hundred dollars from her. "I never touched her money. But it was just like when Denise used to yell at me. It didn't matter what I said, so I just shut up and said sorry.

"But later, I wanted to tell her the truth. I explained about Denise. I tried to tell Barbara that's why I said I took the money, but I didn't take it. She was still mad and she didn't believe me. I could hear her going back upstairs saying, 'Fucking kid!'" He poked at his fries, too stressed to eat. "Now she's going to tell my dad and my aunt and everyone is going to get mad at me. I've never taken money from anybody. You believe me, don't you?"

I had never seen Chris this agitated before, and I didn't know what to think. He was on the verge of tears he was so desperate to be believed. It was like a life-and-death issue for him. I went with my gut feeling and told him I believed him.

The following week, we found out that Chris had used up all his rent money on cigarettes. He just went to the corner store and bought a pack of cigarettes whenever he ran out. It explained where his supply of smokes came from, but it didn't help the atmosphere at the house. Arthur had gone with him to the bank machine and discovered most of his money was gone. "I started punching the wall. Arthur told me to knock it off. He was really mad. I told him I would move out if he wanted. I wanted him to say no but he didn't say anything. I don't know what to do. I don't have anywhere else to go."

I had to admit that I was blindsided by this development. I had assumed that Chris's family was monitoring his bank account — they were certainly micromanaging everything else — but the money issue was less of a concern to me than Chris's reaction to the incident. I could always figure something out — emergency funds from the Ministry or my agency, even getting the family to help — and I couldn't see Barbara kicking him out on the street. On the other hand, Chris was a nervous wreck. He told me that Barbara wasn't talking to him or even looking at him anymore. She had started shutting me out as well: when I tried to ask about her concerns, she would just say everything was fine, she was managing. But I had the sense that she was stuck with something she didn't want to deal with, whether it was Chris himself or his family's pressures. I felt bad for getting her into this. Some new living arrangement was going to have to be made soon. I remembered how excited and proud Chris had been when he'd moved into his own apartment. He didn't deserve to lose all that after trying so hard.

Looking back, I can see that I wasn't paying as much attention to the situation that whole week as I should have been. I was going through a crisis of my own at that time. I was in the process of resigning from my position at Community Services. Thirteen years of casework had finally caught up with me. I was doing transfer summaries on my cases and trying to wrap my head around the idea of leaving a job I loved but couldn't keep up with anymore.

Leaving the agency was one of the most difficult things I had done in my life up till then. The families on my caseload were, in a sense, *my* families: they had opened up to me in ways that many of them never had before, trusted me, and it was so fulfilling to be able to help them get the assistance they needed and deserved. I still miss them.

On the other hand, leaving the agency itself was a greater relief than I had expected it to be. Most of the people I liked had left already, and being there was becoming a bigger strain every day. On my last visit there to clean out my desk, the only person who came up to say goodbye was the receptionist; everyone else sort of pretended they didn't see me. I carried my cardboard box out to my car, wiped the dust of the place from my feet, and hoped I would never see them again.

I stayed involved with Chris as a friend, one who happened to know a lot about case management. He had my phone number, and I guess I thought that should he need to call me, he would. I still wonder if I could have prevented the crisis had I kept in touch during that week before everything fell apart. That kind of regret probably comes with the territory of any helping profession, and it was sheer luck that I had the opportunity to correct my mistake when so many people don't.

On Friday I left a message on Barbara's phone reminding Chris of his appointment with the psychiatrist and asking him to call me back and confirm it. All weekend long, I was uneasy. Chris hadn't gotten back to me and I couldn't shake the feeling that I needed to get hold of him. By Sunday afternoon, the feeling was overwhelming. I called the house again and told Barbara that I needed to talk to Chris.

"He's not here," she said. "He's in the hospital. Didn't you know?"

I felt a shock go up my spine. "What happened?"

"He tried to kill himself Friday night."

Chapter Six

New Uses for a Weed Whacker

Back in the still-functioning section of my mind, it occurred to me to wonder how he had gotten hold of all his medications. A week earlier I had told Barbara to keep them away from him. Apparently, she had given them back. This wasn't a stupid woman, and she'd had a cousin commit suicide two years earlier. What in hell was going on?

"Which hospital?"

"How should I know? Besides, he was just doing it to get attention. You know him."

At some point, I hung up the phone. There were only three hospitals in the area. I called the closest one and got lucky on the first try. Chris was in the intensive care unit.

He was unconscious when I got there, hooked up to IV bottles and monitors. According to the ICU nurse, he'd been comatose since the ambulance brought him in on Friday night. "We nearly lost him. He was awake for a while this morning, but I don't know if you'll be able to talk to him."

I just sat for a while and watched him sleep. He looked about ten years old and so peaceful after all the insanity of the past six months.

It wasn't until much later that Chris told me about the events of the day leading up to his overdose. In the week before his suicide attempt, Barbara and Arthur had hardly spoken to him at all. "I told them I was going for a walk and Arthur said, 'I don't care if you walk to Niagara Falls!' I walked around for about eight or nine hours and I was really tired when I got home. Every time I thought things were going to get better, they just got ruined. I couldn't go through it again. I was thinking about killing myself for a couple days. I kept hoping someone would say something or do something to help, but nothing changed.

"I went in the garage and looked around for something to kill myself with. I thought about hanging myself off the beam going across the ceiling and I pictured them coming in and finding my body. I wanted to be a ghost and haunt the shit out of them. But I couldn't find any rope. There were some chains coiled around in a pile, and I wrapped one around my neck, crossed it in back and just yanked at it." He showed me how he had jerked viciously at the ends of the chain with both hands. "I tried it a couple of times but it wasn't working.

"I tried slicing my throat with a saw blade, but I just couldn't push hard enough. I found an axe, a small one with a red blade, and I thought I could just smash my skull open with it. I took a couple of practice swings," — he pantomimed holding an axe in front of him with both hands and swinging it in toward his forehead — "but I couldn't get enough power into the swing."

"It sounds like you were in there for a long time," I said, trying to sound as calm as I could.

"It must have been hours, I don't know. It was a really long night. I found a chain saw but it was out of gas. Then I picked up a weed whacker from behind the door."

"A *weed whacker*?"

"Yeah, I know, I wasn't thinking too straight. The strange this is, I was kind of laughing and I didn't even know it was me doing it. Finally, I just went downstairs and got my pills. I remember looking at myself in the bathroom mirror. It didn't look like me, my face was beet red and my eyes were bugging out. I looked kind of scary and I remember thinking, 'Good!' I wanted to look like that after I was dead so I could scare the shit out of everybody.

"I put the pill bottles in my pockets and I went out for another walk. I got to a bus shelter a few blocks from the house and dry-swallowed the whole bunch. I just sat there and waited. It was raining hard and I stayed in the shelter and smoked like a madman. I kept waiting and it didn't look like anything was going to happen so I gave up and started walking home. I was about halfway back, walking through this field, and my legs started to go into spasms. I fell flat and just lay there on my back with the rain getting in my eyes and mouth. I couldn't get up. I knew I was going to die and it scared the shit out of me. I didn't want to die. I remember screaming really hard but there weren't any houses or anything near the field. And there wasn't anyone around. I crawled to the road and sat on the curb.

"Then some headlights were shining on me and I heard a car stop and someone get out. This guy came over and shook me on the shoulder. He was black, maybe in his thirties, and he was wearing a suit. He kind of squatted down beside me and asked if I was okay. He said his name was Dublin, or something like that, and he had an accent.

I kind of remember the paramedics coming. When I woke up, I was in a hospital bed. And my dad was there." Chris grinned. "You know, he decided he was an Indian in his last life. One weekend, he even took me to a Native ceremony, with drums and things. I don't know what those other guys were thinking about this fat old white guy sitting in the circle drumming and chanting but it was so fucking funny I nearly choked myself trying not to laugh.

"Anyway, the first time I woke up in the hospital, there was my dad with his medicine drum, banging away and going 'Hey-ya, hey-ya.' I was so embarrassed that I pretended to be asleep until he left."

***

On Chris's third day in hospital, he was awake when I came to visit. The staff were about to discharge him and send him home. He had apparently told them that the overdose was an accident and no one had thought to ask how he could swallow fifty or sixty pills accidentally. I asked to speak to the doctor in charge and, while I was waiting, I asked Chris what was going on.

"I didn't mean to take so many pills, it was just a mistake. I'll be more careful next time. I'm sorry I made so much trouble for everyone." He was watching me intently while he talked. "I wasn't trying to kill myself. You believe me, don't you?"

I took a deep breath and tried to figure out an answer that wasn't going to make the situation worse. Either Chris wanted me to back him up, or he wanted me to call him out about his suicide attempt. I finally went with my gut feeling.

"Chris, you remember our talks about how you need to clear out the garbage in your head that's making you sick?"

He nodded warily.

"Well, I know that things seem to be getting worse. And that's not your fault. It just looks like there's more garbage in there than we realized and it's going to take longer to get well." I smiled encouragingly, I hoped. "Maybe instead of shovelling all that crap out, we're going to have to go in with the heavy equipment and bulldoze it."

Chris grinned but didn't relax his gaze.

"So we're not going to give up and you are going to get well. But we have to deal with what's actually going on here and," — I took another deep breath and plunged in — "yes, I think this was a suicide attempt."

He didn't seem surprised. If anything, he looked a bit relieved.

"You need to tell the doctor the truth. Get a psychiatric evaluation and maybe change your medication to help make you feel better. That's going to mean staying in hospital for a few more days. I don't know if that's what's worrying you, but it's nothing to be afraid of and it's really important to do this."

"My dad and Aunt Olga are going to get mad at me if they think I did this on purpose."

"Honey, I'm sure they're worried about you and they want whatever is going to help you get better. I'll talk to them if it would make you feel better. But you have to tell the doctor the truth."

The doctor arrived just then and I spent the next twenty minutes getting Chris to tell him the truth. Then I had to twist the doctor's arm (almost literally) to get Chris admitted for a psych assessment. Finally, though, he agreed to have Chris sent to the psychiatric ward for observation.

I was confused that Chris was desperate enough to kill himself but not desperate enough to tell his family the truth. It made no sense to me at the time and it was frustrating to be the only one dealing with the reality of an attempted suicide.

I think the question most of us have when people stay in abusive situations is *why?* It's like trying to save someone standing on railway tracks when a train is coming. You rush over to help the person, thinking they're trapped somehow, then you see that they aren't tied down or stuck, they're just standing there. When you try to pull them away from the track, they fight you. You end up walking away, disgusted that the person chooses to be there.

What we don't realize is that, while what we see are train tracks laid on solid ground, the abused person sees those tracks hanging precariously out in midair, like a trestle bridge across some bottomless gulch; they don't see solid ground. When we try to "rescue" them, we're dragging them off the only solid reality they have. It's as if the instinct to survive is twisted and looped back upon itself, like a Möbius strip. The more they want to survive, the more they cooperate with the people who are destroying them.

I'd had clients admitted to in-patient psychiatric facilities and I knew what they were like. Hopefully, Chris wouldn't be freaked out by the locked environment or the other patients. Still, I couldn't help worrying. I hoped I hadn't made things worse.

The next day, I was there as soon as visiting hours started and was relieved to find Chris in his room lounging in his pajamas, perfectly at home. He was happy with the snacks and magazines I had brought and even happier with the pack of cigarettes. He gave me a tour of the ward, starting with the games room.

"They have a pool table and a TV, and you can smoke in there. But I don't use it much. To tell you the truth," he moved closer and lowered his voice, "some of the people in here are crazy."

The last thing you want to do in a locked psych facility is start laughing uncontrollably, but I couldn't help it. Chris, God bless him, had been perfectly serious, but when he realized that he had made a joke, he was pretty proud of himself. We continued the tour through the cafeteria and the outdoor smoking area.

His father (drumless, thank God), his Aunt Olga, and Arthur had all been to see him. I was glad that his family and Barbara's household were being unexpectedly supportive and that several of the financial problems had been ironed out. Chris didn't seem in any rush to leave the hospital, but at least his home environment would be less stressful when he was released.

I asked him if Dana could come with me on my next visit as she had been asking about him. I wasn't sure if he would want people seeing him in there but it turned out he was thrilled to have visitors. So, the next day, Dana and I arrived after lunch. I spotted Chris, all dressed up and waiting for us in the hall.

Chris gave us the tour again and introduced us to a few very interesting people. Dana, not a shy person by any means, was enjoying herself tremendously, exploring the ward with Chris and striking up conversations with other patients. She and Chris went out for a smoke break and, since we knew that Chris would be home by Halloween, she invited him to a costume party at a nearby club. Chris was a fan of horror movies and he decided to be Jason from *Friday the 13th*. He gave us a detailed description of what Jason wore, right down to the colour of his workboots. So, after the visit to the psych ward, we went shopping for a serial killer costume.

On my third visit to Chris, I didn't recognize him. He had gone to the barber the day before and had his head completely shaved. He was excited about his new look, which was going to be part of his Jason persona for the Halloween party. He actually looked pretty sinister and I was picturing the aneurism Aunt Olga would have when she saw him. On the other hand, I saw it as a definite step toward him taking control of his own life. Maybe this was a sign that he was getting better.

Chris came to my house on the night of the Halloween party to get his costume on and left with Dana and her friends. It was his first night home from the hospital and I was up all night waiting to hear how things went. Dana got back from dropping Chris off at his house and reported that he'd spent the evening telling people that he'd just been released from a psych ward and then giving an evil laugh. He was the life of the party. I supposed that was a healthy way of dealing with the whole experience.

But with all the chaos surrounding Chris's suicide attempt and hospitalization, I missed something that would turn out to be crucial. When he was transferred out of the intensive care unit, one of the nurses mentioned to me that Chris had been having seizures of some kind after the drugs wore off. They had sent him for an EEG and an MRI but neither had shown any seizure activity in the brain. At the time, I just assumed that she was talking about Chris's tic, which could get pretty impressive when he was agitated. I found out later that it was something else entirely.

CHAPTER SEVEN

ENOUGH IS ENOUGH

Things seemed better at home for Chris, but this time I wasn't taking any chances. I took Chris to doctor appointments, kept track of his bank account for him, touched base with Barbara frequently and did my best to help keep Chris busy. I hoped that my old agency would be able to set up a residential placement for him soon, but I wanted to make sure that the situation would hold up until then.

He was at my house frequently, hanging out with Dana and her friends, although he often came upstairs to talk to me. I figured he was only being polite. And I still had a feeling that things still weren't going well with Barbara and Arthur. His head-jerking tic would start up as soon as I was driving him home. Chris needed something to keep him out of the house.

I talked to my friend Brynna at the nearby Salvation Army thrift shop and set up a volunteer position for Chris. He loved it there because it felt like working again but with less stress. He would go out on donation pickups and help lift furniture and boxes in and out of the truck. He made friends with the driver, the store manager, and the sales staff. For about two weeks, everything was working out wonderfully, until Barbara, of all people, went in and blew the whole thing up.

Chris was devastated when he called me. I dropped everything and picked him up — he was at the gas station near the Salvation Army store, which was odd. When we got home, I got him a glass of water and sat him down at the kitchen table. He finally calmed down, and I told him to start at the beginning and tell me what had happened.

"When I got to work, I put my lunch in the fridge. But I forgot it was there. So when Brynna asked if I brought my lunch, I said no. She gave me two dollars to go across to the pizza place. My dad was in the store around then, checking up on me. He shows up a lot. I guess he shops there but he would watch me and try to talk to me. That's why I like to work in the back: he can't come back there. Anyway, he saw Brynna give me the money for the pizza and I guess he called Barbara and asked why I didn't have a lunch.

"So I came back with the pizza and my dad said I lied to Brynna just so she would feel sorry for me. He was loud and everyone was looking at us. So I took the pizza and went into the back.

"Then Barbara comes running into the lunchroom with my dad and starts yelling at me for lying and taking money from people. Brynna's there and all the staff are watching us. I'm trying to explain that I just forgot about the lunch, but Barbara's really mad and says I'm just trying to make people feel sorry for me."

Chris looked down, embarrassed. "I started crying, right in front of everybody. I couldn't help it. Barbara said I did that on purpose too, so Brynna would feel sorry for me. Then Brynna told Barbara to leave. My dad went with her but he looked back at me like he'd shown me who was boss.

"Then Brynna told me to go back in the lunchroom and calm down. I stayed in there till everybody was gone, then I went out the back way. I went to the gas station and called you from the payphone. I left my backpack at the store, but I'm not going back for it. I can't go back there."

Chris calmed down after getting through his story. As for me, I was in shock. This was not the Barbara I had known for years. This was some evil twin who was hell-bent on destroying Chris. She knew he was suicidal. What in God's name had possessed her to create a scene like that over a piece of pizza?

But there was still nowhere else for him to go. I kept him at my place for supper and asked if he wanted to spend the night in the spare room downstairs. He reluctantly decided that he had better go home.

Two days later when I was driving Chris to his appointment with his psychiatrist, he seemed keyed up, but we were having a fairly casual conversation — until I mentioned Barbara. He suddenly made a choking noise, bent over in his seat and began having severe, rhythmic muscle spasms. It looked exactly like a grand mal seizure. I managed to get to the curb, then got his seat back and tried to calm him down.

After two or three minutes, the seizure stopped and Chris lay back in his seat, breathing hard and soaked with sweat. From my experience with seizures, I expected him to be unconscious, but he was awake and aware of what had happened. I had a feeling that the best place for him to be right then was at the psychiatrist's office so I stepped on the gas.

Several years earlier I had attended a lecture by Dr. Ruth Ryan of the University of Colorado on the subject of people with both mental illness and intellectual disability. She had described a patient who had suffered from two different types of seizures: typical tonic-clonic (grand mal) seizures and a peculiar type that did not involve loss of consciousness and appeared to be triggered by a specific sound — a train whistle.

It had turned out that this patient had once been attacked and left for dead beside a railroad track and hearing a train whistle would bring back the overwhelming terror of that experience and cause a psychosomatic seizure. Dr. Ryan called the second type a pseudoseizure, and I was pretty sure that Chris had just had one.

When we got to Dr. Vindar's office, I described to her what had just happened. She couldn't explain it but remembered that it had happened before, when she had recently visited Chris in the hospital. That's when I recalled what the ICU nurse had told me about Chris having a seizure. Dr. Vindar suggested that I take Chris home and monitor him.

That evening, Chris had a second seizure. This one lasted longer and Chris had a hard time getting up afterward. I got a friend to help me get him in the car and we went to the hospital. After checking his chart, the doctor admitted him.

I went to see Chris the next morning and found that he was back in the psych ward. The staff neurologist had checked him and found no physiological reasons for the seizures. The staff psychiatrist was confused as well. (Apparently, pseudoseizures are pretty uncommon. I've tried researching them several times as well and found nothing.)

Chris was out on the patio having a smoke when I got there. For the first time, he really looked depressed — not angry, worried, scared, or stressed out, but depressed, as if his batteries had finally run down. I sat down beside him and tried to get him to talk. He made a polite attempt but finally gave up. We sat in silence while he finished his cigarette. Then Chris started to cry. It was a deep, slow sobbing, like something bleeding out from a mortal wound. The sound of it scared the hell out of me.

I put my arm around his shoulder and held him until he could talk again. Other people on the patio were looking at us and I was acutely aware of this. Uncontrolled crying, like uncontrolled laughter, is something you don't want to do much of in a psych ward.

"I can't go back to Barbara's," Chris finally said. "I just can't take any more. Nothing works out, no matter what I do." His voice was different too. It wasn't angry, worried, or even depressed. It had that clarity in it that a person must feel the moment before their boat tips over the edge of a waterfall.

There are moments in life when Fate puts two options in front of you and says, "Choose." You are absolutely free to take either one, and the choice you make will determine not only your life for years to come, but the person you will be while living it. One part of me knew I could keep doing everything I was doing for Chris and it wasn't going to be enough to save him. It wouldn't be my fault and I could spend the rest of my life saying I did my best. The other part of me was just saying, "Fuck it. Enough is enough."

I took Chris by the shoulders. "Would you like to stay at my house until the agency sets up a placement for you?"

I could see that he was trying to get himself to believe it. It was like watching water bead up on soil that had become too dry to absorb it.

"We can set up the cot in the spare room downstairs. I don't think Dana would mind if you share the kitchen and bathroom. You can be roommates and split the rent." As I kept making plans for the move, detail by detail, the reality of it started to soak in. And Chris started planning along with me, becoming more and more animated by the minute.

This was it — this could save him.

By the time I finished the visit, Chris was incandescent with excitement. As I drove home, the reality of it started to soak into *my* brain. I had just taken on a huge responsibility. I pictured telling my husband, Chris's psychotic relatives, Barbara and Arthur, the agency I had just quit and all the other people who were going to think I had gone totally crazy. I tried to figure out how I was going to take care of a very sick young man, day and night, for weeks — maybe months — until a residential placement became available.

Theologians tell us that God sends hardships in order to bring us closer to Him. It works, too. I don't think I ever prayed as hard in my life as I did on that drive home.

Chapter Eight

Room for One More

The first step in Operation Move Chris In was to convince my husband to agree, and that was not going to be easy. Frank was very Italian, and his generosity extended to family, relatives, and friends, but not necessarily to the stray people I brought home now and then.

Frank and I had been married for twenty-five years by this time. We have a solid marriage — we like and respect each other, take care of each other, and have fun together, which is what love looks like in the long term. He's my best friend. But Frank is definitely the boss. He was the oldest son in an immigrant family, his father's right hand, and the authority over his siblings. He left school after tenth grade to help support the family, started a garage business in his early twenties, and had been running it for over thirty years. He's a smart man with a lot of confidence in his own judgment. He's also Calabrese — from the Calabria region in southern Italy — and the Calabrese are known as "testa dura," or hardheads.

When Frank and I started going out together, we happened to watch a movie called *Marty* starring Ernest Borgnine. He kept shaking his head throughout the movie, saying, "My God, that was me!" I could see what he meant:

like Marty, Frank was a heavy man who hadn't had much luck with women. At thirty-six, he had given up on getting married and expected to live with his parents and later with his sister's family for the rest of his life. When we met, he fell in love for the first time in his unsentimental life. I never had any doubt about how much I mattered to him.

And, actually, it has helped even things out between us. Frank is a control freak, but he respects me and he's also scrupulously fair, so we can usually discuss issues. But when push comes to shove, he really hates it when I'm mad at him. I stop talking when I'm angry, and he absolutely cannot take the silent treatment for more than a day or so. I'm not a manipulative person and I don't use it deliberately to get my way, but it did level the playing field several times in the course of our marriage.

But on the drive home from the hospital, I was at a loss for ways to explain my decision to Frank. Honestly, I was a bit freaked out about it myself. Frank had already let me take in Dana after a bad family situation had left her homeless, and we'd known her for years. Frank didn't know Chris at all, and I was bringing him home from a mental ward after a recent suicide attempt. Not good selling points.

I decided to focus on the fact that it would be temporary. Chris was on the waiting list for emergency residential funding, and the agency would be lobbying the Ministry Office to get him prioritized. And Chris would surely be getting better in the meantime — I mean, how long could he stay sick? And, since I'd quit the agency, the extra rent would come in handy.

As I expected, Frank really wasn't happy with the idea. I couldn't blame him for that, but I had to keep my commitment to Chris. There was no choice. After a couple of hours' discussion, he grudgingly agreed. I was relieved, but I knew it was going to cause a lot of tension between us.

Chris moved into my basement directly from the hospital. There wasn't much stuff to move from his old apartment, and Barbara had that packed and ready at the curb when I came by. (I had the feeling it was for either me or the garbage collector, and she didn't much care who took it.)

He seemed thrilled to be there, having Dana and her friends to talk to, and he would act more animated when I was down there. But overall, he seemed to be getting worse instead of better. The first weeks after he moved in, he slept or dozed most of the day. He had a little television and VCR by his bed, and he would play the same movies over and over; when I asked him why, he explained that he couldn't concentrate on a show for more than a few minutes, so he would catch a bit here and a bit there and piece it together. I memorized the dialogue from *The World Is Not Enough*, *Return of the Jedi*, and *The Terminator* during those weeks. And I don't even like those movies!

At night, Chris was a squirming bag of nerves. He was terrified of going to sleep because of the nightmares, and he was afraid to be alone, so I usually stayed up with him until the Ativan knocked him out. Sometimes we were still up at sunrise, talking and telling jokes. As Chris started to relax in his new home, his sense of humour began to surface. He was a natural storyteller and mimic; he did a surreal impression of Yoda having an orgasm. ("Mine, mine, mine, mine, augggh!")

Chris didn't have any more pseudoseizures, but he started having some kind of narcoleptic seizure: several times a day, he would just drop to the ground, unconscious, for as long as two or three minutes. It wasn't safe to leave him alone anymore. We had to watch him on the stairs and listen for him in the shower. Several times, he hit his head on the tile floor or on furniture; oddly, he never felt any pain and there were never any bumps or swelling on his head. When I asked Chris about this, he laughed.

"I don't really feel pain. Look, I'll show you—" He jerked forward and slammed his forehead against the table with a crash that made me jump. Then he sat up with a big grin, like a kid who had just done a magic trick and expected applause from the grown-ups. I checked the table to see if it was still in one piece, then I looked at his forehead — not even a mark.

Chris reported that when he had a drop seizure, it felt like he was pulling out of his body, that he could stand up and look down at himself lying on the ground. He described having a cold, unpleasant feeling when it happened; he was a bit afraid of the whole experience. I had read about children having this feeling (called "dissociating") during abuse episodes. I just couldn't understand why he would be having it now.

I noticed that Chris started stammering when he got nervous. He had done it occasionally before, but it became much more pronounced now. He also started muttering under his breath, repeating a single word over and over again, and would be mystified when it was pointed out to him. Once, the word he repeated was "nipples," which I found mildly amusing; usually, it was more sinister, like "demons" or "Satan."

When Chris had been at my house for about two months, he caught the flu along with the rest of us, but it seemed to hit him harder. He vomited almost constantly. I bought extra-strength Gravol; he threw it up. We got an anti-nausea medication that was usually prescribed to chemotherapy patients; it didn't even slow him down. I began to worry that he might really die if we couldn't stop the vomiting. Chris, on the other hand, was taking it all in stride. I remember one evening when he gave me a big hug, said, "I'm so glad to be here," and toddled off to the bathroom for his thirtieth barf of the day.

One of my friends noticed that his vomiting seemed to have a gagging quality to it; she had seen girls with bulimia self-induce vomiting, and it sounded similar. This made me think of the side effects of Chris's medication, which could include reflux if not taken with food. I made sure he ate before taking his meds; food and meds came up together.

After about a week, I gave up; Chris was dehydrating and he couldn't keep his medication down long enough to absorb it. I took him to the emergency room again. We were becoming regulars: I was spending a small fortune at the Tim Hortons counter, and I had read all the magazines in the waiting room twice. Chris was admitted fairly quickly and put in a bed in one of the exam rooms, and I stayed with him through the night. The doctor hooked him up to an IV to get fluids into him. He added intravenous Gravol, which finally stopped the nausea, at least for the time being. Chris was resting quietly, and we spent the time chatting about all the changes he had gone through in the past two months.

"I'm so happy at your house." Chris held my hands on his chest and covered them with his own. "This is how my mom used to hold my hands so I could go to sleep."

I smiled at him. "You're starting to remember her now. It must have been terrible for you when she died."

"I was eleven. She died six weeks before my twelfth birthday." He looked away for a second. "I didn't know she was that sick. She didn't want to die. Everyone said she wasn't ready to go. She didn't want to leave my sister and me."

I stroked his hair gently. "I think that would be the hardest thing for a mother, to leave her children like that. But I think she would be very proud of you if she could see you now. You've grown up to be a very brave, very good person. Anyone would be proud of a son like you."

He looked at me with an intense expression that I had learned to recognize. "What do you think of me?"

I was startled by the question, and even more startled by my response. "I would be very proud to have a son like you."

His intensity deepened. "There's something I want to tell you. Please don't be mad."

"I won't be mad. I promise."

He drew a deep breath that seemed to suck up all his courage.

"I love you like a mother. Please don't be mad."

What do you say to something like that? And again, I felt the sense that Fate was handing me the choice of two responses. One would be a polite answer, as kind as possible, that I was very flattered, etc., a response that would maintain the distance between helper and helped without making any further commitment. And Chris would accept that, and stay at my place until a residential placement opened up, and then move on, and that would be that. The other choice was a full commitment, something that I might be taking on for the rest of my life.

I sucked up all my courage: "I love you like a son."

The strangest feeling came over me then, a feeling like something had finally come into focus. I remembered a quote by Frederick Buechner: "The place God calls you to is the place where your deep gladness and the world's deep hunger meet." This was it, then, the place that I had been heading toward since I had met Chris, maybe since I had started as a social worker, maybe all my life. It felt ... right.

Chris lay back on the gurney with a completely contented look. "My stomach's quiet now."

"How long have you been thinking about this?"

"About a week. I kept trying to get up the courage to tell you, but I kept chickening out. I've been shitting bricks worrying about it. I mean, it could have gone really wrong. What if I had said I loved you and you had said 'WHAT!?' I would have been really screwed."

"Maybe this is what you have been throwing up over?"

Chris grinned. "Maybe."

The doctor came in a few minutes later and removed the IV: they were discharging him. The social worker who had brought him in a few hours ago was now officially retired. Chris was finally going home with his mother.

CHAPTER NINE

BLAST FROM THE PAST

The next day, Chris had his first flashback.

I had taken him to the walk-in clinic to get his asthma checked out. He was in a wonderful mood. We were joking about his habit of apologizing constantly; he decided to go for a Guinness World Record, and I kept count. (His record stands at thirty apologies in sixty seconds, but we haven't checked with Guinness yet.) The clinic doctor was very nice but not fluent in English, so Chris pantomimed an asthma attack for him and finally got a prescription. As we went next door to the pharmacy, Chris started to get quiet and preoccupied. After we got the medications, he said that he needed to go home. In the car, he began to wheeze; I handed him the new asthma inhaler, but it wasn't doing much good. When we got home, I put him to bed downstairs and left him to take a nap.

About an hour later, Dana came up to get me; Chris was in his bedroom, moaning and shaking, and didn't seem to know where he was. When I got to his room, he was cowering in the corner at the foot of his bed, completely disoriented, staring around the room in absolute terror. I sat down on the edge of the bed and tried to talk to him, asking him where he was and who I was; he didn't seem to hear me. Then I tried to calm him down, telling him he was safe and everything was okay, but I may as well have talked to the wall. Wherever Chris was, he wasn't with us, and wherever he was, he was definitely not enjoying it. And I had no idea of how to get him back.

Finally, I climbed over to him, got him around the shoulders in a bear hug, and started to talk right into his ear as loudly as I could without deafening him: "Chris, it's okay. You're safe. Nothing's wrong. You're all right. Everything's okay." I kept repeating it over and over, until I could feel his body start to unclench. He looked at me, and then around at the room as if to orient himself, like someone who had just awakened from a nightmare.

"Chris, are you all right? What just happened?"

"It was like some dream or something, but I couldn't break out of it. I could hear you calling me, but it was like you were miles away. I kind of followed your voice back."

"Chris, I nearly broke your eardrum. You really couldn't hear me?"

He shook his head, exhausted. I got him to lie back down, told Dana to watch him, and then ran upstairs for the sublingual Ativan (a tranquilizer pill that dissolves under the tongue and gets into the system in about fifteen minutes instead of the forty minutes it takes regular pills). I was picturing another trip to the emergency room. Chris took a hefty dose of the meds, then settled back to let it take effect. I went back upstairs to explain to my husband what all the yelling was about.

When I came back to check on him, Chris was huddled on the edge of the bed, sobbing. Sitting down beside him, I put an arm around his shoulder and rocked him. He took a deep breath to get the words out: "Evelyn! We were in love, we were going to get married when we grew up! Ursula took her away from me! I lost her, I lost all my friends, because of Ursula!"

After the Ativan started to take effect, Chris was able to explain what he had been upset about. "When I moved to Ottawa, I met a girl named Evelyn. My stepmother found out about her and started telling her lies about me. Ursula told Evelyn and all my friends that I had raped her, and she showed them naked pictures of herself to prove it."

"Where did Ursula get naked pictures of herself?"

Chris stopped for a second, confused. "My ... my dad took them. I told my friends not to listen to her, she was lying, but they all believed her. Evelyn wouldn't talk to me anymore. It got all over school.

"Ursula showed them pictures of my dog Sasha with her head in my lap and told everyone that I was doing something perverted with the dog. I kept trying to tell them that I was just giving her a dog biscuit, but that got all over school too. I went to one of my classes and there was a stuffed animal on my desk, and one of the guys said it was something to keep me busy until I got home. I got so mad that I threw it at him, and then I just cut school and went home. I tried to kill myself that day, I got a knife out of the kitchen and took it into my bedroom and tried to cut my throat. I cut enough for it to bleed, but I couldn't make myself push hard enough."

"A grown woman talking like this to a bunch of kids, and showing them naked pictures of herself? Didn't any of them think that was weird?"

"I don't know. They just seemed to believe her."

Chris was exhausted, and the tranquilizers were really kicking in. He lay down on the cot, and I stayed by him until he fell asleep. So this was what it would be like when he started to remember his past. I was more sure than ever about

Ursula; a woman who would show naked pictures of herself to kids would probably do more. She seemed to have been trying to keep Chris isolated, which would also fit the pattern of an abuser. So what was going to happen when *those* memories showed up?

With Christmas on the way, we seemed to get some respite from any more symptoms for a while. Chris was invited to visit his mother's family in Timmins for a week, spending Christmas with them for the first time in ten years. Plane tickets were really cheap for some reason that year, so he was even able to fly there and back. Chris was thrilled to be on an airplane again, and I was relieved that the trip would only take a couple of hours.

Focusing on preparations for the trip significantly reduced Chris's fainting and vomiting (which still happened when he was nervous). I did notice another side of his personality, however: when Chris looked forward to something, he obsessed about it to the point of exhaustion. He used to worry about bad things happening, in a resigned sort of way. But when he got his teeth into anticipating something good, he was like a terrier with an old shoe. It was as if he had to keep thinking about it and talking about it to make sure it would actually happen.

While we shopped for presents for every family member (and Chris must have been related to half of Timmins), he spent hours reminiscing about his childhood. He had an encyclopedic memory for names, birthdates, addresses, and other details embedded in these early memories: "So my Aunt Elise, she was married to Uncle Charles, they got married in 1953, she was sixteen and he was eighteen, their last name is Delon, they had two children, George in 1954, then Julie in 1956, Julie is married to my cousin Louis, he's just my cousin by marriage, their last name is Langnard even though he doesn't speak French, they got married in 1975, he had a moustache then but he shaved it off after, actually he looked better with the moustache, they had my second cousins Janet and Roger, Janet is a year older than me and Roger is two years younger, he was born in June 1982..."

We also went through Chris's photo albums. His mother had put them together, and Chris translated some of the captions from French to English for me. He remembered an idyllic childhood centred around his mother and sister, with frequent visits by doting relatives and friends. But I was struck by something in his childhood photos: he wasn't smiling in any of them. He was the most sombre child I had ever seen. One photo particularly disturbed me: he was about two years old, looking into the camera. I had heard of the "thousand-yard stare" that combat soldiers get after too many battles; it was unnerving to see that stare in the eyes of a toddler.

The photos stopped at around the time Chris was eight. I remembered that his mother had died when he was eleven, and wondered if this was when she first got sick.

"I don't remember her being sick. She did cough a lot, like this," Chris demonstrated with a deep, phlegmy growl, "but we just got used to it. I don't remember anything else about it. When she went to the hospital for the last time, she told us she was coming home soon. We had Christmas at Sarah's house, and the next day my dad told us that she was dead."

"Your mother died on *Christmas*?" This sounded like something straight out of a Dickens novel.

"The day after. I never liked Christmas after that. But this Christmas is going to be pretty good, seeing all my family again. I can't wait to go on a plane again, too. When my mom was alive, we went on vacations every year, and we flew a lot of times. She took us to Disney World, and Nashville once, and I can't remember where else…"

When the day arrived, I saw Chris off at the airport with all the anxiety of an overprotective mother. I didn't exactly pin a note to his jacket, but I made sure he had our phone number, his Aunt Babette's number, his tickets, some emergency money — I spent so much time on the checklist that he nearly missed the flight. With all that had happened in the six months since his last visit, I wasn't sure Chris was ready for this trip — or that his relatives were ready for the new Chris.

Chris came home a week later with a big smile and a pile of photographs. He went over every minute of his visit, describing each of his relatives in detail and every conversation verbatim. This Christmas had been the kind he remembered from his childhood, with midnight mass on Christmas Eve followed by a party called a *réveillon* at his aunt's house where the gifts were exchanged. He even got to spend time with his grandmother, who at ninety-six years old was still alert and healthy and telling him dirty jokes when her daughters weren't around.

Strangely, none of Chris's symptoms had followed him to Timmins. He ate normally, and didn't vomit once during the visit. There were no nightmares, no drop seizures, no flashbacks — nothing. Chris hadn't really thought about it, but I was amazed. What could have caused this hiatus in his symptoms? And, more importantly, would it last?

Chris had felt very much at home, except for one thing. The whole family was francophone, and Chris had been fluent in French until he was twelve. But when he went home, he couldn't understand any of his relatives unless they spoke English. Obviously, he hadn't had much chance to practise his French in Ottawa with an English-speaking father, but his losing all his comprehension of his first language was odd.

It reminded me of an article I had read in university about people who grew up bilingual. They often did not translate well from one language to another. My husband, for instance, grew up bilingual but had a terrible time translating family conversations for me. I finally decided to learn Italian myself, and it surprised him when I was able to translate words and phrases from one language to another so easily. (It surprised me that I still couldn't understand a word his family was saying after two semesters of night classes. That's when he casually mentioned that his family doesn't actually speak Italian; they use a Calabrese dialect that is only spoken in their home village. I can't believe I've stayed married to this man.)

In this study, a group of bilingual adults were given personality tests in each of their fluent languages; they scored differently in each language, as if they had different personalities depending on the language spoken. One explanation for this was that bilingual people may compartmentalize their personalities in order to accommodate the different cultural experiences connected with each language. I wondered if "Francophone Chris" had been tucked away after his mother's death. If someone like Chris had buried his memories of his childhood, would his childhood language be buried along with it? And would the language come back if the memories did?

CHAPTER TEN

WHAT HAPPENS AT TIMMY'S...

Although his symptoms returned after Christmas, Chris still felt happier than he had in months. He felt safe and in control of his life for the first time in years. He seemed to be taking things in stride, and he was even hoping to start work again soon. To me, it felt like the calm before the storm.

For one thing, the Zombie Mom nightmares were becoming more intense and graphic. Sometimes after he told me about a dream, I couldn't believe that he hadn't clued in to the obvious message. But he definitely hadn't. During one of our talks, he told me, "I've been through almost everything except being molested. I'm glad about that, anyway. I don't think I could have handled it."

I nearly choked on my tongue. Chris was being absolutely sincere; he had no idea of what was about to come out of that black hole in his mind. Should I tell him, or let him recover the memory on his own?

The crisis finally came two weeks later. The setting was, of all places, a Tim Hortons. He was telling me about his latest Zombie Mom dream over crullers and hot chocolate, when he had to go to the men's room for his regularly scheduled barf. (I often wondered how the other customers felt about hearing someone being violently ill in a restaurant bathroom. Chris was probably responsible for a lot of Health Department inspections. I still believe he closed down the Burger King across the street.)

When he came back, his mood was different; it felt like the buildup of barometric pressure before a thunderstorm. He sat for a moment, playing with his paper cup. "These dreams are getting to me. I wish I could just make them stop." He glanced up at me, with what I had learned to recognize as his "fill in the blank" look. He was giving me an opening, and I figured it was time to take it.

"Chris, you know who the Zombie Mom is, right? It could only be Ursula. I mean, that feels like the right answer to you, right?"

He nodded warily, watching me as if I were about to explode.

"And the dreams are about Zombie Mom kissing you and lying on top of you, and it all feels really gross and sick the whole time?"

Chris nodded again. I had a moment of insight: he knew where this was going. He just needed me to go ahead of him. I took a deep breath.

"Okay. I've been thinking for a while now that the dreams were about Ursula. And the way you feel in the dream is probably the way a child would feel about being molested. I think Ursula sexually abused you."

We were both silent for a moment. The issue was finally on the table, sitting there among donut crumbs and crumpled napkins.

Chris looked calm, even relieved. "I think maybe you're right. I don't remember anything, but she could have done something like that. I could see her doing it, she was sick enough. I really hate her."

I felt pretty relieved, too. This had gone better than I had hoped. "Do you want to go home? It might be a better place to talk about it."

Chris glanced around at the nearby tables out of the corner of his eye. "Yeah, let's go home."

We picked up the table trash, found the garbage bin, and headed out the door. By the time we got into the car, Chris was starting to hyperventilate. When I asked what was wrong, he didn't hear me. His eyes seemed to be staring inward, at some private horror. "The coffin is coming out of the ground ... the dirt is flying up out of the grave... Now the coffin is up on the grass ... the lid's creaking ... it's starting to open..."

I drove the few blocks back to the house with one hand on the wheel and the other holding Chris down. He was rearing up out of the seat, straining at the seatbelt straps as if he was trying to rip them off the bolts. His eyes were nearly bulging out of their sockets. "There's something inside...it's scratching to get out...it's smashing the lid... THE COFFIN'S OPEN!!!!... THE COFFIN'S OPEN!!!... IT'S GETTING OUT!!!!... IT'S OUT!!!!"

PART II

CHRIS

The child trapped in an abusive environment [...] must find a way to preserve a sense of trust in people who are untrustworthy, safety in a situation that is unsafe, control in a situation that is terrifyingly unpredictable, power in a situation of helplessness.

—Judith Lewis Herman

Chapter Eleven

Childhood's End

North Bay still haunts me. I was born there, and it's the only place I remember being happy. I still wonder how my life would be right now if I never moved away, and none of the other things happened. I would have grown up around all my friends and relatives. I would probably have a job and a family, like everybody else. I would be normal.

My mom was from northern Ontario; her family had been farmers and miners in the area for over a hundred years. We all spoke French at home, except for my dad. My sister Janice and I had the kind of childhood you see in reruns of old TV shows: we lived in a neighborhood where we knew everybody, and we spent holidays with our relatives. Mom always wanted to have kids, so she stopped working so she could stay home and take care of us. I remember it as a really happy time.

Everybody loved my mom. She was really small, under five feet tall, but she had a big smile and a big heart. She was good to everybody, and she was always helping people. She was a good cook — she had been a dietician for twenty years — and she would bring meals over to neighbours when they were having hard times.

I loved my mom's cooking. She did a lot of baking, from scratch, and she let me help. She taught me to cook my first meal; it was eggs, and I had to stand on a chair so I was even with the stove. Once or twice a week, my mom would make my favourite supper, steakspaghettigravy — plain spaghetti noodles with steak and gravy on top.

I remember when my sister was little. I can still see her toddling over to me with her arms up for a hug, and the memory breaks my heart. I thought she was so beautiful; my mom took a picture of me in her crib putting cold cream on her face to make her pretty. I was cradling her face and she looked like a teeny circus clown. My mom took another photo of us making "toilet stew": we would pour shampoo and things in the toilet and stir it with the scrubber brush, then we'd flush and watch the bubbles.

Another time we burned out my mom's new vacuum cleaner. I found out that we could feed it toilet paper and it would make the whole roll unravel and disappear. I showed Janice how, and we took turns. I think we fed it about six or seven rolls. My mom must have heard the vacuum running, because she called out, "*Que'est-ce que tu fais?*" ("What are you doing?"), and I called back "*Rien!*" ("Nothing!") But then the motor on the vacuum started to smoke, and we both started screaming for Mom. She was pretty mad that time. She had to buy another vacuum cleaner.

Our house in North Bay was built when I was a baby. I have a photo of us moving in, and my mom was holding me in her arms by the front door. It was a beautiful place on a small lake, with a back that sloped down so you could walk out to the backyard from the basement. It was like being out in the woods. My mom made stew for supper once, and we all sat out on the big boulder near the lake and ate the stew. It was like camping out.

My mom's family lived nearby, by Northern standards — about two hours' drive — so we visited them all the time, and stayed for a few days at a time. I loved these visits. My first cousins were all older, some with kids my age. There was always someone to play with, and the adults spoiled us all. My Aunt Michelle and Uncle Charles had three children. Sophie used to dress me in doll clothes when I was a baby, and moved on to Janice when I got too big. Lucy's daughter, Aimée, was born when I was five, and I have a picture of Janice and me trying to feed her in her high chair — we were wearing most of the food. Marc was a teenage headbanger, with long black hair down his back and his very own motorcycle. He introduced me to heavy metal music before I could pronounce "Metallica," and I've listened to it ever since.

Mémère and Pépère, my grandmother and grandfather, lived near Aunt Michelle. They were in their seventies but still kept up the family home, and Pépère still drove the family car. (When he was ninety he hit a mailbox and had his licence taken away, and he never got over it. For the next eight years, all he talked about was how much he missed driving.)

My Aunt Claire and Uncle Pierre lived further north, in a paper-mill town. When they first married, Uncle Pierre had worked in the nickel mines like the rest of the family. He was in an explosion that crushed half his skull; he ended up with a steel plate in his head and a glass eye, and no workman's compensation. Aunt Claire was pregnant with my cousin Richard, and she went deaf at around the same time. After some hard years, Uncle Pierre found a job at a paper mill, and moved the family north. He built his own house there, one of the first in the town, and my cousin Richard and his son Albert still work at the same paper mill.

Uncle Pierre and Aunt Claire were interesting to visit. She could read lips, in French and English. He would tease us by taking out his glass eye and telling us, "I've got my *eye* on you!" They had grandchildren by then, which meant second cousins to play with. Their daughter Renée ran a chip truck, and we got free hot dogs and fries whenever we wanted. The town smelled funny because it was so close to the mill, but we got used to it.

The memories of my dad are the dark side of my childhood. I never thought of him as a father; he was always the Mean Man. I spent my childhood wishing he would die and leave us alone.

My dad's family came to Canada from Hungary when he was about eight years old. The Communists were taking over Hungary then; my dad and Aunt Olga were only children at the time, but he remembers seeing men with machine guns at his house. They moved to Toronto, and my grandfather started his own business making airplane parts, and eventually became a millionaire. I remember my grandfather being a lot more strict than my mother's relatives, but my dad said that his father used to yell at them all the time, and he remembers seeing his father beating his mother. I never met my real grandmother because she died before I was born.

My dad got a degree in Chemistry at university and went to work for DuPont at one of their factories. He was married once before my mom, and he told me that he decided he would never beat his wife the way his father did — but he ended up beating her anyway. They got divorced, and then he met my mom. My parents were married when she was thirty-seven and he was thirty-two, and five years later I was born.

What I remember most from my childhood is Janice and me hiding downstairs and listening to my father screaming at my mother upstairs in the bedroom. Sometimes we'd hear banging or my mom saying, "Stop it, Eddie, that hurts!" I remember thinking that, sooner or later, Daddy was going to kill Mommy.

I was also pretty sure that, sooner or later, Daddy was going to kill me.

When I started school, one of my dad's obsessions was teaching me arithmetic. He would sit me down at the kitchen table and every time I got an answer wrong, he would yell at me or hit me. Once he sent me flying and the chair fell over. I told him, "Daddy, you hate me." He said, "I don't hate you, I love you, but you are going to get this goddamn thing right!" I still have a mental block about doing arithmetic. Just looking at numbers makes me nervous.

Dad was unpredictable, especially if he was in a bad mood. He liked kicking me, maybe because I was too short to hit without bending over. Once, I was walking through the living room and my dad was sitting on the sofa. He said to me, "I'm a barbarian." I thought he was joking, so I said, "Aw, come on, Daddy." He got up and started kicking me in the ribs, and just kept kicking and kicking until I thought my ribs would break. When he stopped, I went up to my room. It hurt to breathe, but I couldn't stop crying. My mom heard me, and she came in to ask what was wrong. I showed her my ribs, and she went downstairs and screamed at him, "Don't you ever touch my son again, you son of a bitch, or I'll kill you!" I was thinking, "Go on, Mommy, yell at the Mean Man!" Then she came upstairs and looked at my ribs to see if I needed to go to the hospital. She ran a tub of cold water and gave me a bath to take the swelling down.

At night, I would listen for his footsteps, for the door to swing open, for him to come roaring into my room. Once he grabbed my cheeks and pulled them so hard that I thought he was going to rip my face off. Another time, he lifted me off the bed by my throat and pinned me against the wall with my feet dangling in the air.

Only Janice was safe from our dad. He doted on her. He never yelled at her or hit her. I wasn't jealous of her; actually, I was glad he didn't hurt my baby sister. She was Daddy's girl and I was Mommy's boy. That's just how it was in our house.

Every family has its version of "normal," and that was ours. It was a hard life in some ways, and a happy life in others. We were pretty well off. I had a lot of toys, and a lot of friends, and we went on family vacations a lot. I loved staying in hotels on our trips because Janice and I could go swimming in the hotel pools. My favourite of all our vacations was to Disney World in Florida.

My mom and aunts told me that I had a terrible time holding down food as a baby; I didn't cry much, but I threw up a lot. When I was a toddler, I was terrified of using the bathroom: my mom had to stand guard in the doorway for me. I could never sleep without the lights on, and I still can't.

I loved school, but I had a hard time learning; I remember that I had to go out of the class for part of the day to get extra help. My aunts would tell my mother that I was "slow." This would really upset my mom. She would tell her sisters, "My Chris is a genius!" At home, I could solve Rubik's cubes and Transformers all by myself. I came up with my own superhero costumes: for He-Man, I wore a pair of suspenders backwards, put a pair of underwear on over my pants, and pulled on a pair of yellow rainboots. Batman was easy: my Batman Underoos, a towel, and my toy carpenter's belt. I never felt stupid; it was just hard to concentrate enough to learn stuff.

Even after my mom started to get sick, things stayed normal most of the time. She would tell us that she was going to get better, and we would believe her. Then I would hear her coughing really hard or spitting blood in the toilet, and I would get a really weird feeling. And it would be scary when she had to go to St. Michael's Hospital in Toronto for treatments. Sometimes we all went and stayed with Aunt Olga in Mississauga; then it was like visiting relatives and I could forget why we were there. We would go sightseeing in Toronto and play with our cousins, and then my mom would be out of the hospital and we would go home. Other times, she would go without us, and all we had were babysitters and my dad at home. Those times it was harder to believe that things were okay.

Even with the lung cancer, my mom still smoked. I remember that I started to smoke when I was nine, about a year after she got sick — not a lot, but I think that it was to make sure that if she did die, I was going too. The idea of staying behind with my dad was unthinkable.

My dad wasn't much help to us, and I didn't expect him to be. But there were times when he found a way to make things even worse. I remember one car trip back from Toronto — I was about ten, I think — and my dad was crying and telling my mom that he couldn't carry on without her. Janice and I were in the back seat, and my dad looked over his shoulder and told me that he would have to give us away because he wouldn't be able to take care of us. I started bawling — not because I wanted to stay with him, but because I didn't want to be away from my mom.

The truth is, I still believed that my dad would end up killing me sooner or later. My mother was the only protector

I had, even if she couldn't protect herself from him very well. He still bullied her, no matter how sick she was. One of my best memories of her was after my dad sent her to her room. He really told her to go to her room, like she was a child, and she did. After he went downstairs, I opened the door and asked her, "Are you all right?"

She was sitting by the bedroom window that looked out over the lake. "I'm fine, honey."

"What are you doing?"

"Just looking at the boats." I went over to stand beside her, and we watched the sailboats together for the rest of the afternoon.

Mom had cancer for three years, and the changes were so slow that I guess we got used to them. The year I turned eleven, there were times when Mom was too weak to take care of us. Sometimes a neighbour would help out, and sometimes my Aunt Claire would stay at our house for a few weeks. But Mom still told us not to worry, she would get better, and I believed her. So I wasn't prepared for what happened at Christmas.

That year, we were having Christmas dinner with Sarah's family; she was our neighbour from across the street, and I was best friends with her kids, Tom and Teresa-Lynn. Actually, I had my first crush on Teresa-Lynn, but I was really shy about it. My mom had helped take care of the kids when Sarah's husband had been in the hospital with a stroke, and Sarah had helped us out later on, when my mom was getting sicker.

After supper, we were all playing downstairs when they called the ambulance for my mom; her skin looked grey. Before she left, she told me, "Don't worry, honey, it will be fine. I'll be in the hospital for a few days, and then I'll be home." Those were the last words she ever said to me.

My dad went to the hospital with her, so we stayed overnight at Sarah's house. The next morning, my dad came home and told us that my mom was an angel. I didn't get it at first, but then Janice started screaming and I realized what happened. Janice was crying, and I hugged her and told her that everything was going to be okay, but it just wasn't real to me. She wasn't really dead; it was a mistake.

We went back to our house, and I kept waiting for my mom to call from the hospital. My aunts and uncles came to stay with us, and I wondered why everyone was so upset. I was like that for days, until we went to the funeral home. The casket was closed — there was no viewing or anything — but I realized that my mother was inside that box, and she was never coming back. Then everything was real, and it was like my whole world fell to shreds. The funeral was the next day, and I cried all the way through it. Since it was winter and the ground was frozen, my mother couldn't be buried. The family took her body to Astorville in the spring and laid her in the family graveyard. I never saw her grave; by then, I was in Ottawa.

We had been planning the move before my mom died. I hated the "For Sale" sign on our lawn, and I'd tear it out of the ground and hide it when no one was looking. The house was sold anyway. My dad had a new job in Ottawa, and we all went there to look for a new home. I hated the whole idea; my life was in North Bay with all my friends, and my relatives, and my school.

We moved out of the house about three weeks after the funeral and stayed at a hotel for a few days while the movers packed up our belongings. Janice and I invited our friends over to the hotel to swim in the indoor pool. I remember going over to my friend Jamie's house to say goodbye just before we left, and I must have had some kind of breakdown.

Jamie's mother had been friends with my mom. She told my dad that I needed some mothering in order to heal from my mom's death, and she offered to keep me for a few weeks. I stayed behind in North Bay while my dad and sister went on to Ottawa. I spent time with Jamie's family like I was a part of it, and I fantasized about staying there and being adopted. It didn't happen, though.

I remember when Jamie's mom put me on the bus to Ottawa at the end of the summer. We were both crying. I kept saying that I didn't want to leave. She bought me fries and gravy, and told me that everything would be okay. But I knew it wouldn't. It felt worse than dying to get on that bus, and I cried the whole way to Ottawa. I was going to go live in a strange place, and there was nothing to protect me from my dad anymore. Sooner or later he was going to kill me.

CHAPTER TWELVE

THE EVIL STEPMOTHER

Our new house was a really big two-storey building with a kidney-shaped pool in the backyard. It was a nice house, and I liked it, but it wasn't home. My dad had hired a live-in nanny named Justine to take care of us, but she wasn't my mother. I spent the first three weeks in the new house up in my room, crying and saying I wanted to go home. I don't remember anyone coming up to check on me.

I was still in sixth grade, and it was probably March when I started going to my new school, St. Therese. It was a French-language school, like the one in North Bay. That was when I lost my French; I couldn't understand what the teachers were saying. I couldn't do my lessons or follow along in class. The other kids spoke to me in English, but I didn't try to make friends: my friends were all in North Bay, and these were all strangers. After a few weeks, they transferred me to an English school across the street from my house. I still didn't want to make friends. It felt like I was losing who I was, and it was a creepy feeling.

I began to feel completely alone, too. All my life, Janice had been the person closest to me, after my mom. Now she seemed to block me off like everybody else. My dad had told me that one day I might come home and everybody would be gone; the idea terrified me. Then one day I came home and the house was empty. I went from room to room screaming, until my dad, Justine, and Janice popped out of the kitchen pantry and laughed at me. My dad's behaviour was no surprise, but it hurt to see Janice going along with it.

Then, that summer, my dad started to date Ursula.

Ursula Delgado was short, like my mom, but kind of scrawny. She was from Honduras, and she still spoke with a heavy Spanish accent. She was divorced, she said, because her husband had abused her. Her kids were in high school; Julio was fourteen, three years younger than Jacinta, who already had boyfriends. Ursula was working as a massage therapist when she met my dad. They dated for the summer, and then my dad asked me how I would feel if he married her.

I told him, "Do what feels right for you." My mother had been dead for seven months, and he wanted to get married again. It was creepy in a way, but I didn't really care what he did. So Ursula and her kids moved in with us that summer.

At first it was okay; I liked Jacinta and Julio, and Ursula treated me nicely. Janice and Jacinta became like best friends. I thought that Ursula could even become like a mom to us. She used to call me "*mi amorcito*" like a pet name; my mom had called me pet names, too.

Ursula and my dad got married that summer, right before I started seventh grade at St. Peter's. I don't remember much about the wedding except that it was in a big church and that I met Ursula's sisters. But after that, Ursula started getting friendlier, touching me more and calling me "sexy." I didn't like it, but who could I tell?

It was harder than ever to concentrate, and I had a stammer then, and the other kids made fun of it. My voice was starting to change around that time too, and it would go from normal to squeaky without warning. I didn't know what was happening, and I was scared that I was going to lose my voice. That was about the time I was getting an attitude, too: I was angry all the time, and I would threaten to punch other kids in the mouth when they teased me.

By that time, life at the new house was hell on earth. My dad was working as an explosives technician and was away from home a lot. Ursula would take me into the hot tub in the master bedroom, and she would get naked and make me take off my underwear. Then she would touch me on the privates, and she would grab my hand and make me touch her breasts and her privates. I would tell her, "What are you doing, you should be doing this stuff with my dad."

"Your dad's not here. Don't you like me to do these things?"

"No. It's gross."

"Why, don't you like me?"

"NO!"

"Oh, you hurt my feelings. That's okay, I forgive you."

When she was finished, before she let me leave, she would wave her finger at me and say, "Remember, don't tell anybody." That was before she started threatening to kill me.

By my thirteenth birthday, I was smoking up regularly. Pot kind of relieved all the anger for a while, and it helped me forget about what was happening — and I really needed to, because by that time Ursula was forcing me to have sex with her. She was also starting to tie me up and do things to hurt me while she was raping me. That was when she bought a gun — a custom silver-plated 38-calibre six-shooter.

Ursula would take photographs and videotapes of the rape sessions. After she was finished with me, I'd lie on my bed and listen through the wall as she played the tapes in the master bedroom. I could hear myself crying and Ursula telling me to shut the fuck up.

I was starting to feel like I wasn't even human anymore. At school, I'd sit in class with all these kids that had normal lives and loving families, and I'd feel like an alien. I'd ride home on the bus and listen to their plans to do stuff that night; then I'd go home, take some food up to my room, spend the whole evening smoking up, and wait for everyone to go to bed and Ursula to knock on the door.

And I couldn't even turn to my sister. I remember she and Jacinta were having friends over for a party, and Janice asked me to take our dog Sunny up to my room and keep her out of the way. So the dog and I sat upstairs in my bedroom and listened to my sister partying with her new family and friends.

I tried to get through to Janice once after that. I still believed that, no matter what was going on, deep down she was my sister and she would help me. I called her into my room, closed the door, and sat down with her. I told her, "Ursula is raping me."

Janice stood up, looked at me, and said, "Get real!" Then she left. We never talked about it again. But that was the end. I didn't have a sister anymore.

Life was very confusing. At night, when Ursula was raping me, I knew who the bad guy was. But during the day, she would become the "good mother" and I was the "awful child" who did everything wrong. She told me I was stupid and mentally subnormal, that my mother probably died of shame for having a cripple like me for a son. Even though I knew what a sick bitch she was, the things she said still hurt me a lot. I was ashamed of what Ursula was doing to me, I was ashamed of using drugs, and doing badly in school, and being so angry and full of hate that I couldn't think straight. And that wasn't who I really was.

I tried to make up for things when I joined Boy Scouts that year. Eddie had mentioned that there was a scout troop starting at Mayflower Elementary School, and I thought it might be interesting, so I walked over and signed myself up. I worked like a madman to earn badges, and over the next two years I got nearly every badge that the Scouts offered. I even got Bronze, Silver, and Gold stars and rank chains for my sash. I learned to sew them on myself, and they were my prize possessions. I felt normal when I was out doing stuff with the troop. One of the best times we had was winter camp, when we learned to build snow huts. My friends Rob LaBelle and John Beck and I made our hut with a hole in the roof, and we went inside and smoked cigarettes without the troop leaders catching us.

One day, Ursula showed up at one of my troop meetings, and I knew something bad was going to happen. I was getting a badge that night, and she sat through the ceremony with this little smile on her face. After the meeting, she went up to the troop leaders, Franco and Ian, and I saw them looking at me. They called me over and told me that I was out of the Troop. They wouldn't tell me what Ursula had said.

The next day, when I came home from school, Ursula had been burning garbage in a metal barrel in back of the house. My Scout uniform and sash, with all my badges, were in the barrel, and there was nothing left of them except burned rags. I went up to my bedroom and got stoned. I didn't cry about things anymore.

I had a collection of car models that I put together from kits. I did all the gluing and painting myself. I kept them in my room. I came home from school one day, and Ursula had trashed my room and broken all my models. I never did another one, and I still can't.

About this time, my dad was starting to drink a lot. I mean *a lot*. His study was on the same floor as the bedrooms, and he stayed in there all night, he even slept in there after a while. He also got this weird idea that he'd been in Vietnam as a special ops soldier. He got these tapes of marching music at an army surplus store, and all night long I'd hear him play his army music, pounding on the desk or marching back and forth. Then he'd stop for a while, and I'd hear him mumbling to himself. Then the music would start again, and this would go on all night until he passed out.

One Saturday, I had a friend over and we were in the kitchen making french fries, and my dad came marching down the stairs naked. "It's a great day, boys! A great day for *the Marines!*" Then he turned around and marched back upstairs. My buddy and I cracked up, but it was still pretty embarrassing.

It was ridiculous sometimes, but other times he was pretty fucking scary. One night I was in my room playing my music, and he told me he would set me on fire if I didn't turn that noise down. I turned off my music; when he left, I crawled under my bed and slept there. Another time, I was just falling asleep when he opened my bedroom door. He had his boomerang knife in his hands, it had a great big curved blade, it was the kind they used in Indonesia to kill water buffalo. His eyes were bugging out like he was crazy. He didn't say anything, and I just sat there, I couldn't move. Then he closed the door and went up the hall, and I went under the bed again. The next morning, I went into the tool shed and got a small chainsaw; I oiled it and put gas in it, and brought it up to my bedroom. I kept that chainsaw under my bed for months.

CHAPTER THIRTEEN

PORKY PIG STRIKES BACK

Grade nine was when I became a rapper. I went to school the first day in my preppy clothes, and I met these guys named Jason and Ricky who were listening to rap music. I liked rap by then, so we started talking. The next day, they took me shopping for Exhaust jeans, boxer shorts, big T-shirts, high-top runners, and baseball caps. I went home and burned all my sissy clothes. My family didn't know what to make of the new me.

Piercings were a part of the rapper style too, and I decided that I wanted a couple of earrings. I tried piercing my ear with a needle and an ice cube, but I couldn't get the point all the way through, and it bled like crazy. Ursula finally paid to get two studs done on my left earlobe; later on, I got two small gold hoops.

I bought piles of rap CDs and started trying to rap. I wasn't great at it: "I shot that big fat bitch, there was nothing else to do so I threw him in the ditch…" My favourite artists were the Wu Tang Clan and Old Dirty Bastard. All the swearing and violence in the songs were a way to get some of the anger out of my head.

We were the stoners at school, and I even started dealing a bit, just to cover expenses. I kind of remember going to classes late, really mellow, and it must have been pretty obvious. The kids around me kept giggling and whispering, "Hey, Chris is stoned!" The teachers didn't do much since I didn't cause any real trouble in class. I went through Visine by the gallon, and Febreze to get rid of the pot smell, so my family didn't catch on for a long time.

After school, I'd go over to friends' houses and get high. I learned how to make a B-52, which is pot and crack burning in a pop can; when you inhale from the can, you get blasted. I liked skunk weed, a kind of pot that stinks but gets you really high. The weirdest experiences came from cartoon acid, a type of LSD that makes you hallucinate cartoon characters. Usually it's a pretty funny trip, but this one time, I was walking home at night and I hallucinated Porky Pig chasing after me with a butcher knife. I started running like hell, while all the lampposts began bouncing and singing "Zip-a-Dee-Doo-Dah." It sounds funny now, but I was scared to death.

I also got laid a lot. There were a lot of girls in our group, and I was considered pretty hot. We switched around; some girl would be in love with me one week, and in bed with my best friend the next, so it was better not to take it too seriously or you would be in fights all the time. I had one friend, Elise, who had a steady boyfriend. He got her pregnant and dumped her. She had a baby boy, and I would go over and help her take care of him. He was so cute, I couldn't see how anyone wouldn't want to be a father. I would have loved to find a girl, get married, have a baby, and get the fuck away from my sick family.

Most of the kids I hung out with had pretty bad home lives. Jason would show me his bruise marks, and I'd show him mine. Our gang was more like a family than our families were: we liked and respected each other, and we felt safe in our group.

I can't remember how I happened to start seeing a psychiatrist; somebody from the school must have suggested it or something. Anyway, around my fourteenth birthday, I took a bus to the Children's Hospital of Eastern Ontario to have an interview with Dr. Agnew. I can't remember most of the interview, but I remember her asking about whether I was being abused. I couldn't tell her about the sexual abuse, but I did tell her that my dad was physically and emotionally abusing me. Dr. Agnew wrote this stuff down, and then suggested that I come to a teen outpatient group that she was running.

The group met after school two or three times a week. There were six or seven of us, boys and girls, all about the same age. We would have group, then cooking class, then gym. I was shy in group, and most of the other kids talked about getting into fights and beating people up. Cooking class was okay, but I ditched gym a lot; I thought the other kids might make fun of me and I'd get mad, and it just wasn't worth it. The program didn't do me much good, I just went to keep people's mouths shut. Some of the kids were okay, but I didn't get to know them well. I didn't like it much, the atmosphere was too tense, it didn't feel safe to open up.

I went for a couple of months, then I got discharged, meaning I didn't need it anymore. I kind of hoped they might have helped me, but I didn't really care.

Some time later, I was in auto body class when my muscles stiffened up and my eyes rolled back. Ursula came and drove me to the hospital, and brought me inside in a wheelchair. The doctors examined me, then made me lie down on the sofa; they pulled my pants down and stuck a big needle in my butt cheek. It hurt like hell, and I was swearing at them and at Ursula. She told the doctors I was having trouble sleeping. They decided to keep me overnight. I was in a hospital room by myself; Ursula stayed for about an hour, and Eddie came by that evening with some stupid comic books. It was a long night; I hated being there, and I needed to get out and smoke up. I was feeling really lightheaded from the drug; everything felt like a dream. I couldn't sleep, so I went out to the patient lounge, where there was this really old lady in a wheelchair. She looked way too fragile, almost like a skeleton, I felt like something was wrong. I tried to talk to her, but she didn't say anything. I finally asked her name, and she said "Rachel" in this weak little voice. I had to go to the bathroom; when I came out, she was gone. I hadn't been out of the room long enough for anyone to take her anywhere, but nobody was in the halls or anything. I even asked the nurse at the desk if there was an old lady named Rachel on the ward, and she said there wasn't anybody like that. It was creepy. I went down to the smoker's patio and smoked like a madman until morning.

After the hospital, it was like a switch got flicked on inside me. I felt homicidal. I really wanted to kill everyone in the house. One night, I got a butcher knife from the kitchen and went to Ursula's room. I held the knife an inch from her throat while she was sleeping, and I gripped it until my knuckles were white. I kept thinking, "Don't do it, they'll lock you up and never let you out." I finally gave up and put the knife back.

One night, I cried all night, I knew I was losing my mind and there was nothing I could do about it. Early in the morning, I went downstairs; Janice was down in the kitchen, and she came into the living room and saw me. I was still crying, and I told her, "Ursula's driving me crazy."

She said, "Chris, calm down. I'll make you some breakfast." And she did. It must have scared her to see me like that, though, because later she told me that she was having dreams of me coming after her with a knife.

The anger slowly started to quiet down, for about a month or two. Then Ursula did something to reignite the feelings, I can't remember what, but I told her, "I could kill you right now, you know." Something in the way I said it must have scared her, because she had me readmitted to the hospital. They kept me for two days, and nobody came to visit. That was a good thing, because I would have killed them. It was like putting a match to gasoline: the feelings blazed up and burned hot, even my face was red from it. I can't believe I kept myself from murdering them. When I had those feelings, I felt my soul had left. I wasn't Chris anymore. I felt like a true killer, all I wanted to do was murder, I wouldn't even have felt any remorse.

Back when I had left North Bay, there was a little bit of myself left inside, a piece that still had some happiness. Anger accelerated the change in me: there was no happiness left. I felt like a full-blown monster in human form.

I started fighting at school and got a reputation as someone you didn't want to fuck with. When I got mad, I'd actually see another face on that person — my dad's face. The first time it happened, it was like — *blip* — and the face changed, and I was kind of freaked out, but then I just went after the guy like I was going to kill him. After that, every time I got in a fight it was my dad that I was beating up.

Still, there were guys who tried to kick my ass, maybe because I was small. It didn't matter, because I had an insane tolerance for pain. I remember one time at school I was in the boys' bathroom taking a piss, and four guys came in. Paul, the biggest of them, said, "Hey, this is my place, get out."

I wasn't done, so I said, "I don't see your name on it, maybe I should write it for you — in piss."

He came at me, and drove his fist into my crotch. I calmly said, "That's a pussy shot, you chickenshit." Then he caught me in the mouth. My teeth were bloody, but he didn't loosen any. I pulled back and nailed him in the side of the head, and he went down. I turned to the other three, but they ran out on him. I went to the door, there was a latch on the inside and I locked it. I went to the sink and rinsed the blood out of my mouth. Then I beat the living shit out of the guy. He really thought I was going to kill him. I thought so, too.

Marijuana was the only way I could control the rage. It calmed me down enough to keep from killing. But I had to smoke myself into oblivion. Two joints didn't do it: I smoked five or six, I kept smoking until I couldn't remember my own name.

The summer I turned fourteen, we all went to Honduras for the summer to stay with Ursula's family. That summer probably saved my sanity; it was the vacation I needed from my life in Ottawa. It was also when I got my wisdom teeth pulled by that dentist, but other than that it was a great summer. We were near the beach, and I went swimming every day. We were staying with Ursula's mother and sisters, so she couldn't do anything to me at night. She would give me these warning glances, though, not to say anything to anyone. Her family were all really nice people, I couldn't figure out how she had turned out so twisted.

That was when I learned to drive. Ursula's nephew Roberto used to hang out with Julio, they were both about sixteen, but sometimes he would take me out in his mom's car. It was a 1994 candy-apple-red Honda Civic hatchback with a standard clutch. The first time, I thought I was going to kill us both. Then I got the hang of it. They don't have speed limits or stoplights in Honduras, at least not where Ursula's family lived. I remember driving down the freeway at seventy miles an hour, feeling like Bo Duke driving the General Lee.

When we got back from Honduras, the house seemed different, more evil. I felt like, shit, no more already. About two nights after we got back, Ursula started raping me again.

CHAPTER FOURTEEN

LIVING AND LEARNING

Ursula had been taping the rape sessions, but I never thought anybody else would see the tapes. I mean, she wouldn't be stupid enough to let people know what she was doing to me. So it shocked the hell out of me when I found out she was selling copies of the tapes. I saw her selling a tape to some neighbours, about four houses up the street. Another time, she took me in the car with her to deliver some tapes to another customer.

That was bad enough. But my first day of ninth grade, I went into my science class and saw my teacher hiding a black VHS tape and giving me a guilty look. I knew what was on that tape.

Mr. Merckle was a tall, skinny, nerdy-looking guy who looked like he was born to teach high school science. He had this high, nasal voice, which got annoying really fast, and he blinked all the time, like it was some kind of tic. He knew that I knew; and when nothing happened, I guess he felt brave and started getting in my face. He would keep me after class and tell me what he thought of the tapes. He had bought three of them from Ursula. He told me that he masturbated to them.

During class, it was a different situation. Mr. Merckle was always riding me and humiliating me in front of the class. He sent me to detention a lot, which was fine with me because I didn't want to be in his fucking classroom.

But this one time, I guess I'd had enough. I got an answer wrong and Mr. Merckle wouldn't let up. Even the other kids were looking at me like they thought this was weird. Finally I snapped. We sat at small tables in his classroom instead of desks. I stood up, sending my chair sliding back, and picked up the table. I threw it at him. The table flew across the room and hit the blackboard. The table legs had these little flat feet on the bottom, and one of the feet stuck in the blackboard. The table just hung there on the wall for a few seconds. Then it came loose and hit the floor with a big crash.

First, I asked the other kids, "Is anybody hurt?" Nobody was, but they were all staring at me in shock. Then I turned to Mr. Merckle, who was hiding behind his desk by now. I headed for him, I could hear him begging, "Now, Chris, there's no need for this. We can work things out."

Before I reached him, the door opened and another teacher rushed in and asked if anything was wrong. He must have heard the table fall. Mr. Merckle told him everything was okay. I just walked out of the classroom. That was the last time he harassed me.

Around this time, my dad went to work drunk and got fired. He really lost it after that. He would stay up all night getting drunk and screaming at the top of his lungs. He threatened to kill everyone in the house. We all started to sleep downstairs in the basement, on the pull-out couch or in sleeping bags. I can't remember how long it went on, but it was several weeks, maybe a few months.

Neighbours must have called the cops sometimes, because every now and then they would show up. They'd go upstairs and talk him down. Afterward, he would come downstairs and hug me and say, "Don't be scared of your crazy old dad." I'd just look at him and not say anything. I hated him so much by then that nothing he did mattered.

Then Eddie made the mistake of hitting Ursula. She was sleeping downstairs with the rest of us, but she didn't seem as scared as we were. She would laugh when the screaming started upstairs and say, "Well, there's your crazy father again."

I think it was a Saturday morning, I was in the kitchen having breakfast when Ursula tried sneaking into the master bedroom to get dressed. I heard some banging around, but I didn't think anything of it. Then Ursula came downstairs holding her face: "Your dad just beat me!" She had a black eye beginning to swell up. I just started crying, I was so sick of all the violence. I went downstairs to watch television. Janice called the cops.

They arrested Eddie in his boxer shorts and sandals. I watched them slap the cuffs on him, and I loved it. I loved watching him leave. I was thinking, "Take Ursula too, then it will be perfect." I wanted to say something to the cops, I was standing right next to one of them, but Ursula was keeping her eye on me.

I went upstairs to Eddie's room, and it was disgusting. He had crapped his bed. I changed his sheets, then I noticed the mirror on his bureau. He had put little yellow sticky notes all over it: "Bitch." "Fucking bitch." "Bitch."

Eddie was in a detention facility for a few months, I don't remember how long, but nobody went to visit him. When he did come home, it was like, "Aw, fuck, you're back." He wasn't drinking then, and he tried to suck up to Janice and me.

Once, he wanted to take me out for donuts and hot chocolate. I told him, "*No — fucking — way — fucking — ever! Fuck!*"

He went upstairs, and then my sister Janice came down. "You know, Dad's trying. You could be a little nicer to him." I couldn't believe it: she was sticking up for him. Then he came down. He was crying, and it just turned my stomach. I went out for donuts with him just to shut everybody up.

He told me, "It wasn't my fault, your stepmother was driving me crazy. She said things ... they were unspeakable. That's what drove me crazy." I didn't want to hear any more. I couldn't believe that he wanted *me* to feel sorry for *him*. He was supposed to be the parent, and worry about his kids. It just made me hate him more.

He didn't stay very long. He and Ursula separated after a month or so and got divorced a little while later. Janice and I stayed at the house with Ursula. My grandfather spent a lot of money getting Eddie set up in his own place, an old run-down apartment about five miles away from us. It was the first time he had ever lived on his own: he had always either lived with his parents or one of his wives. He still wasn't drinking, but he was as much of a bastard as ever.

With all the shit happening at home, I was doing really badly at school. I think the only classes I was passing were woodshop and auto body — I actually got a certificate of achievement for body work and painting, and I was thinking about this as a career. It was easier to concentrate when I was working with my hands.

Sometime in the spring, I got tested by a psychologist at school. They pulled me out of all my regular classes, even the shop classes, and I was sent to the dummy class. I lost a lot of my friends, because all the Living and Learning classes only had the special ed students in them. I was completely humiliated.

The only good thing about the Living and Learning program was my new social worker, Mrs. LaSalle. She was in her forties, with black hair and really kind eyes. I used to have talks with her every day about things that were bothering me. I told her that my dad was an asshole, but I never mentioned the sexual abuse; by then, I had given up hoping to be believed or rescued. It was just easier not to expect help.

She knew that I used drugs, but didn't push me on it. The only thing she wanted was for me to stay in school and not give up. She was the only person who seemed to care about me, to be concerned about whether or not I self-destructed. I knew it was her job, but it still felt good to matter to someone.

One of the teachers in the Living and Learning program seemed really nice at first. Mrs. Atkins was kind of chubby, with short hair and glasses. She always wore an apron because she taught the pottery class, as well as other stuff. When a new student joined the program a little while after me, Mrs. Atkins asked me to give him some extra help.

Troy was in a wheelchair; his legs had been paralyzed in a car accident. He seemed like an okay guy, so I agreed to be his assistant, but it turned out Troy was a manipulative asshole on wheels. He ordered me around, made me pay for his lunch and buy things for him. And he was really good at making people feel sorry for him. When I hung out with my friends at lunchtime, he would wheel himself over and watch me with a miserable look on his face until I gave up and went back to him. When I sat with my girlfriend, he would come over and interrupt us. I would tell him to piss off, and then she would get mad at me for yelling at this poor handicapped boy — and he would play it for all it was worth. I kept telling her that she didn't know what he was really like, but she wouldn't listen.

I was told that Troy could go to the bathroom by himself, and he could really, but he started making me help him. Then he told me to jerk him off.

"No fucking way!"

"You better do what I tell you, or I'll get you in trouble with Mrs. Atkins."

"How about I tell Mrs. Atkins what you just asked me to do?"

"Go ahead and tell. She says she supports me getting you to do this for me."

"Bullshit, I'm telling her."

I went to Mrs. Atkins, the classroom teacher, and believe it or not, she wanted me to do it. "Troy is in his teens just like you, Chris, and he has a hard time getting girlfriends. I think you could help him out with this a little."

"And what if I don't want to?"

"I would like you to do as I ask, and if you don't I can start some rumours about you. It could ruin you at school. It would be easier if you would just help out a little."

I didn't have a choice, I started jerking Troy off in the handicapped washroom by our class. I didn't go to any of the other teachers after the talk with Mrs. Atkins; none of them would have believed me over her.

Once, Troy told me that Mrs. Atkins listened at the door. I didn't believe him; I pulled the bathroom door open, and she was standing right there.

At lunchtime, she would take Troy and me to an abandoned portable classroom in the back of the school, and watch me do stuff with him. I could see that she was getting off on it. I think she had some kind of sick crush on Troy; she was always really nice to him in class, and called him "sweetie" and stuff, but this was really gross.

The only friends I had were my druggie buddies, and I hung out with them all the time now. Some of my friends dealt dope, and they asked me if I wanted to get into dealing regularly — it was good money. But I told them, "No fucking way I'm keeping that shit at my house! My stepmom would kill me." I got a Pennysaver paper route to pay for my drugs and cigarettes, as well as my new clothes and CDs. I didn't mind the job; it was just a couple of hours a few times a week, and it was an excuse to get out of the house.

I only smoked outside of the house, or in my room by the window; I had poked a hole in the screen to get rid of the butts and ashes. Then Janice saw me smoking with some buddies by my schoolyard. She went to a different school, and her bus just happened to pass by at the wrong time. She put the bus window, leaned out, and called to me, "You're dead! You're dead!" Sure enough, as soon as I got home, I was in deep shit from Ursula. I was grounded for days.

A week later, I was out with one of my buddies when he was making a sale, and Ursula drove by and saw me. I recognized her red Presidia, and I figured I was going to get yelled at again. Instead, by the time I got home, there was a police car by the house: Ursula had called the cops on me, and had me arrested for drug dealing. This would have been a good time to tell the cops what Ursula had been doing to me, but I never said a word. I spent four or five days in detention, I don't remember exactly how many. I was in with some bigger kids, and a couple of them made me do stuff. There wasn't much I could do about it then, but later on I ran into one of them on the street, and I beat him to a bloody pulp.

It was about this time that I started shoplifting. It was just candy bars from the K-Mart near my house, but it felt good. I was so full anger by then, and I was sick of being a victim. There were days that I would come home from school and stand across the street from my home, and just look at it and hate it; I would stand there for half an hour sometimes, thinking, "I hate that house and everyone in it."

I finally got caught stealing a four-pack of candy bars. The security guard from the K-Mart chased me out of the store, but I got over a chain-link fence and thought I'd lost him. He grabbed me when I was almost home and marched me back to the store. I was so mad, I told him that if I had a knife I would stab him in the neck. He just looked disgusted with me.

Ursula picked me up from the store security office. She was really angry. When we got home, she sat me down on a kitchen chair. She turned on one of the elements on the kitchen stove and waited until it was bright red. I was confused: did she want to cook something? Suddenly, she grabbed my wrist and pulled my hand over the stove. I struggled as she tried to put my hand on the red-hot burner. Then I put my foot up against the oven and shoved backward. I elbowed Ursula in the stomach as I got away, and she fell to the floor. I felt bad about that, but I wasn't sticking around to pick her up; I ran out the back door and stayed at a friend's house that night. That was the last time she ever laid a hand on me.

After that, Ursula decided that I needed to go live with my father. Eddie had a one-bedroom apartment, and when I stayed overnight I slept on the sofa-bed. He was staying sober, and the apartment was reasonably clean. I was glad to be away from that damned house and everybody who lived there, but moving in with Eddie would not have been my solution. I would rather have moved in with friends or even on my own, but that wasn't possible at my age. So, a few months after my fifteenth birthday, I moved in with my father.

CHAPTER FIFTEEN

SK8R BOI

One good thing about Eddie is that he didn't keep tabs on me like Ursula did. I had a lot more freedom. I could keep my drugs in the apartment, and I even brought my girlfriend over a few times when he wasn't there. I was using the sofa bed in the living room, so it wasn't very private. Once, he nearly walked in on us: she slid under the bed, and hid for almost an hour until he went into his bedroom. She was giggling, and I was giggling, and I can't believe he didn't notice anything, but he didn't. I figure the drinking had killed off a lot of brain cells.

Eddie didn't do much grocery shopping or laundry. I was doing most of the housekeeping and I took my own clothes to the laundromat; I was fucking well not going to do his laundry for him. I stole money from his wallet for groceries and cigarettes, and I learned to cook a bit. It was kind of like having my own place.

Even when Eddie wasn't drinking, he was always calling me "Stupid," "Moron," "Dough-head!" It got old fast. I started yelling back, and that shook him up a bit. I also stayed out most of the time with my friends. He was also out of the apartment a lot — I don't know where, because he still didn't have a job, but I didn't really give a fuck.

At the end of tenth grade, we moved into a two-bedroom apartment. I liked having my own room again. The apartment was a decent-looking place; it was in an older building down in the Bayshore area, one of the bad parts of Ottawa. A lot of drug dealers and fights. I fit right in.

I went out exploring the neighbourhood as soon as we moved in. There were a lot of kids my age, and I made friends fast. I spent all my time hanging out at Bayshore Shopping Centre with my new crew, and came home when I felt like it. After living with Ursula, it felt like getting out of prison. I felt so much better about things. I started bathing more often, kept my clothes washed and ironed, and learned how to shave by watching my dad from the bathroom door.

Most of the kids around Bayshore were into skateboarding, and I decided to try it out. My grandfather sent me some money, and I spent it on an Alien Workshop board and trucks. I put my board together by myself, and my new buddy Dave taught me to use it. I bought a few pairs of Airwalk skateboard shoes and new clothes. One of the main differences between a rapper outfit and a skater outfit was the wallet on a chain, and I made my own with a dog leash, two metal keychain links, and a wallet that I hole-punched an opening through. I also got a skater haircut — shaved around the sides and back, long on top. I usually wore it with the long part in a ponytail, but I could gel it into liberty spikes or a mohawk when I wanted to. I still hung out with my rapper friends, but I started getting back into heavy metal. Headbanger music, like Megadeth and Metallica, was a good outlet for my anger.

I never got great at skateboarding, but I could do a few stunts. Once I pulled a slide off the top of a park bench, and found myself in midair. For a second I was thinking, "Oh, shit, I'm gonna faceplant." But I controlled my fear, grabbed the board, and held it out to my side. I got it back under my feet just before I landed, and my gang went crazy. My girlfriend whispered, "You are so going to get laid tonight!" It was a good day.

One day my buddy Dave was showing off, trying to rail-slide down a really high railing at the Bayshore Shopping Centre parking lot. The board broke in half, and he fell and hit his mouth on the concrete. His mouth was full of blood, it was everywhere, all over his clothes. I helped him home. His parents were really mad, but they got him to a dentist. The next time I saw him, his mouth looked okay, but he was kind of traumatized.

Eddie had been exploring the neighbourhood too. There was a small bar called Crackers about a block away from the apartment, and he started hanging out there. I remember him taking me there for supper one night. The food was pretty good, and I had a burger and some poutine. Then I noticed the pitcher of beer beside Eddie's plate, and I thought, "Aw, shit!" I knew what was going to happen.

Sure enough, three nights later, Eddie came home stinking drunk, and started screaming "Fuck! Fuck! Fuck!" He went in the kitchen and started opening and slamming the cupboard doors. I can't believe the neighbours didn't call the cops. I went downstairs and slept on the sofa in the apartment lobby until I was sure he had passed out.

At Bayshore, I met Jesse and Drake, two hardcore drug dealers. Jesse's dad was in prison, and Drake lived in a group home. Like most of my gang, I bought from Jesse and Drake. After they had known me for a while, they asked me if I would like to make some extra money. It seemed that my old drug dealer friends had been telling their connections that I'd been arrested for dealing and hadn't ratted on them. This meant that I had respect from the other dealers. Jesse offered me a middleman position, meaning that I would buy from him and sell to the lower-level dealers. It meant a lot of money and a lot of respect. I told him I would do it.

I wasn't worried about getting caught the way I had been at Ursula's place. Eddie was too wasted to catch on, as if he even cared what I did. I dealt pot, hash, and crack, but no hard stuff. The money was crazy good, and I started saving up for some things, like shoes and jeans and new boards.

And a gun.

I'd wanted a gun for a while, and it made a lot of sense if I was going to carry drugs or money to some of the places where I would be dealing. I had a jackknife, but it wasn't much protection. But it was more than that. It meant power, not being anybody's bitch ever again.

I wanted a pistol because they're more powerful than revolvers. A Beretta would be the best, but any pistol would be okay. And it had to be black.

Jesse knew some gun dealers, so he checked around for me. Nobody had a Beretta, but he could get me a good pistol for eight hundred dollars. He didn't ask what I wanted it for, you don't do that. I gave him the money, and about three weeks later he called me.

"I got it. Come over now, and I'll show you how to clean and load it."

I felt like it was Christmas morning I was so excited. I biked over to Jesse's house, and there it was: big, black, ten rounds to the clip. Jesse showed me how to take it apart, clean it, reassemble it, load the clips, and aim and fire. I couldn't stop smiling at the gun. Jesse laughed at me. "You're gonna be really obsessed with this gun for a while, aren't you?" He gave me some ammo and a couple of extra clips, and told me that he could get me more if I needed it.

I biked home with the gun, and I felt taller, my balls felt bigger. When I got home, I took a shower. I stood in front of the mirror in my boxers and felt myself changing, getting colder and angrier and more powerful. I felt like a super villain. From now on, *I* was the asshole, *I* was the one that other people were going to be afraid of. I wouldn't hurt any women, children, or animals, I wasn't going that far, and I wasn't going to be an asshole to my friends. But the next time Eddie fucked with me, instead of "You might kill me," it would be "*I* might kill *you!*"

I bought an adidas knapsack, and that was my gun bag. I didn't take the gun to school, but I carried it everywhere else with me. I slept with it under my pillow: I always used two pillows, and the gun was on the bottom, with the clip between the pillows. I pictured Eddie coming into my room with that fucking boomerang knife one night; I would pull the gun out, slam in the clip, and unload it right in his face. I even figured the time it would take for him to get across the room with the knife, and how long it would take for me to load and aim.

The next time Eddie came home drunk, he started yelling at me. I ignored him, and he threw a punch at me. I grabbed his shirt with both hands and slammed him against the wall. "You've hit me for the last fucking time. I hit back from now on, and if you keep this shit up, I might have something that will make you fucking dead." His eyes got really wide, and he looked almost sober when I let him go. He went to his room, and I never heard a sound from him that night. After that, he would still come home drunk and loud, but he wouldn't try to beat me up anymore.

Having that gun seemed to change my personality. Even my face changed: my expression looked cold, kind of creepy, like there was nothing inside. And that was just how I felt: I sincerely didn't give a fuck.

I got in a lot of fights, but now I started them. It was business: if someone disrespected me or shortchanged me, I had to do something about it or I was a pussy. Most of the time, I just beat the guy up. But there was this one dealer, a big Jamaican dude, who kept shorting me and running his mouth about it. I got him alone, and held my gun to his head. He had diarrhea in his pants, I swear to God. I told him, "What is that fucking smell? I can't believe you did that. Look, I don't want to kill you if I don't have to, but I'm teaching you a lesson." So I shot him in the foot. When he went to the hospital, he told the doctors that he shot himself by accident. That was the biggest rule: you don't rat.

Another time, Drake and I beat up this guy who had shorted Drake a few times. We got him on the ground and kicked him, just kept kicking him. I was ready to stop, but Drake kept going. I was afraid he was really going to kill this guy. I kept telling him, "That's enough! *That's enough!*" He didn't even hear me. Finally, I pulled my gun out and put it to his head. "STOP IT NOW!" He stopped. The guy we beat up was an awful mess, missing teeth and everything, and I still feel bad when I think about it.

One time I really enjoyed my new asshole abilities was when my old classmate Troy became a customer.

Troy had moved into a building in the Bayshore area that was set up for wheelchairs. Troy had also developed a crack habit, and he got my name from another customer. When I recognized him, I couldn't believe he had the balls to call me after what he had done to me in school. Troy tried to pretend it hadn't happened and get buddy-buddy with me. I got really cold-blooded with him: "You better get one thing straight right now. I'm here to make money off you. I am not your friend; and if you can't remember that, I know how to make sure that you don't forget." I pulled out my pistol, loaded it, and cocked it right in front of him. He shut up, paid, and I left.

I actually started enjoying having Troy as a client. I made a lot of money off him: the guy smoked four or five rocks a day, at fifty bucks a rock. I also loved watching what the drugs were doing to him. He was turning into such a crackhead it was pathetic. I could tease him with the drugs until he cried like a baby. Payback is one beautiful bitch.

My life was kind of split down the middle between my school friends and my dealer buddies. I kept my drug dealing away from my friends, because I didn't want them mixed up in all the violence. I even had girlfriends who had no idea that I was a heavy-duty dealer. I sold drugs at school, at lunchtime under the bleachers or in the trees beside the school; but I never carried my gun or wore my rings and chains at school. When I hung out with my friends, I could let down a bit, but even they noticed the change in me. My best friend, Elise, the one with the baby, told me that I seemed really cold. I just shrugged.

Actually, I hated school by then. I couldn't concentrate, I was too pissed off all the time, and the Living and Learning class was for mentally slow students and was kind of boring. But I stuck it out because I wanted to get my diploma and make something of my life. I wasn't going to be a criminal forever, I just didn't have many options as a fifteen-year-old. I remember another drug dealer I met at Jesse's place: he had a *college education*! I flipped out on him: "Man, what the fuck are you doing dealing drugs with a college education! You could get a real job, you could do anything! Do you think I'd be doing this shit if I could go to college? I'd have my own business and be making legitimate money. What kind of *fucking loser* are you?!" He just stared at me. I guess he wasn't expecting that from someone like me.

I used to think about what would happen when I graduated. I wanted to go into the military. I wanted to shoot people and blow shit up. I didn't think much beyond that. But I did join the Air Cadets. We met two or three times per week, learning marching drills and studying aircraft and munitions in class. I was promoted to corporal and then to sergeant. I led drills and taught classes, and I was a real SOB. I got a kick out of being hard on the other cadets. The other sergeant, my superior, was twenty-two; he told me that I was a vicious little bastard but that I was good at what I did. I was sure that Air Cadets was going to lead into a spot in the Air Force. When I found out that it didn't, I started to lose interest. All we did was the same drilling and shit every week. I started skipping meetings, and eventually, I quit. Drug dealing was taking up more of my time by then.

Hanging out with my dealer buddies was a different kind of relationship. It wasn't exactly friendship, since we couldn't really trust each other, and there was always the possibility that you were going to have to beat somebody up for business reasons. But it was sort of a brotherhood: we had each other's backs, and we could let down about being in the drug business, which we had to keep quiet about everywhere else. It was kind of like *The Sopranos*, only not that hardcore.

We partied all the time. Jesse had a two-bedroom apartment of his own: he was twenty-two, even though he looked like a teen. His room had an extra bed and the spare room had two sofas, so people could crash there if they wanted to. I sometimes packed a change of clothes and spent the whole weekend there, getting high and hanging out with the crowd. Jesse had one rule: you could bring your gun, but you had to unload your clip. We weren't really into fighting, actually — that was business. Most of our violence was directed toward customers who didn't pay.

I didn't get drunk very often, but at this one party there was a lot of hard liquor and I couldn't stop. I found a kid's pedal car in the apartment, and I got in and pedaled it up and down the hallway yelling, "Don't drive impaired!" I kept drinking until Jesse finally stopped me. I stuck to pot and beer after that.

Keeping my two lives separate — school friends and druggies — was getting harder, and part of it was that I was changing. I was taking anger to a whole new level, and it was a part of every relationship, whether I meant it to be or not. One day, I got in an argument with Elise, and she told me to hit her. I was horrified: it never occurred to me to hit a woman, no matter what. I told her that, and then she told me that her old boyfriend, the baby's father, used to hit her, even when she was pregnant. That lit my fuse. I knew where this guy lived; I told Elise that I had a gun and I was going to go over to his house and empty ten rounds in his face. She told me that she didn't want to be friends with me anymore, that I had changed too much. I got up and told her to fuck right off if she didn't like who I was. Then I left. I still regret losing that friendship, and wonder how she and her son are doing. The boy would probably be in his teens now.

When I was sixteen, I met a girl named Carlita. She was a year younger than me, and really hot. She had red hair and freckles, and was kind of short, which was perfect for me. I liked Carlita, but she had a crazy side. We got into an argument once when I was taking a bath. She brought a toaster into the bathroom, plugged it in, and threw it in the tub. I jumped out in time, but I got such a powerful shock that I ached in every muscle for hours. I got mad at her, but we didn't break up over it. I still don't understand why.

Carlita broke up with me after about three months. She caught me dealing drugs and threatening a customer with my gun. I think it scared her. It wasn't that big a thing. I really liked her, but it wasn't love. I never let any of my girlfriends get that close.

Part of it was keeping them away from the drug-dealing, keeping them safe. But there was so much else I couldn't tell them — about Ursula and the abuse. Most of all, though, I was so full of anger that there wasn't room to feel much else.

Except maybe one thing. I used to hang out at the Bayshore Shopping Centre a lot. Every now and then, a family would come along with kids my age or younger, and you could tell they were happy together. I'd just watch, and maybe nod or say hi; but when they passed, I would look after them with absolute hate. Then I'd go home and cry myself sick. After that, I would smoke up like I wanted to erase my whole existence.

Drugs were starting to take their toll, though. One day, I would be partying with Jesse; the next day, he would be holding a gun to my head because I was short a hundred dollars on my collections. Jesse was on crack now, and he smoked up constantly. It was changing his personality the same way anger was changing mine.

Things came to a head when I was short a few ounces of skunkweed in one of the bags I brought back to Jesse. He got furious, phoned me and told me he was coming over to kill me. I pulled out my dad's boomerang knife and waited for him. When he arrived, I met him in the stairwell across from my apartment.

He had his gun out, and he cocked it and pointed it at my forehead. "This is it. I am sick of your shit. You shorted me for the last time. I am going to fucking blow your head off."

"Go ahead. Do it." I meant it, too. I honestly didn't care at that point.

Jesse stopped, with the gun still pointed at my head.

"Go on, pull the trigger. You think I'm scared? Go ahead, kill me."

Jesse dropped the gun down to his side. It was still cocked, but he looked stunned. I just got madder. I knocked off his baseball cap, grabbed his hair, and pulled his head down. I held the boomerang knife against his throat. "You pussy, you couldn't even pull the trigger. I could cut your throat right now and leave you in the stairwell. Nobody would even know until they fell over your body."

He didn't move. I just felt sick of the whole thing, and I let go of his hair. "It was three fucking ounces. You have bags of the shit at your place. What the fuck?"

We both just stood there for a moment. I told him, "I'll make good on the three ounces of weed tomorrow. I'll see you at your place." I walked out of the stairwell and into my apartment. I put away the boomerang knife before Eddie got home. Then I smoked up to soften the adrenaline rush that was still burning through my system. The next day, I brought over the weed that I owed Jesse. Neither of us ever talked about what had happened.

What happened to my friend Melissa finally got me out of drug dealing. She knew what I did, and she needed money to get away from an abusive home. She asked me to help her deal some drugs. I tried to explain how dangerous the drug business was, but she was determined to get into it. So I introduced her to Jesse.

Melissa wasn't good at business, and she came up short twice. About two or three hundred dollars each time, which was pretty bad. Jesse let it slide the first time. The second time, I knew there was going to be trouble.

Jesse drove a white Mazda, and I recognized it when he pulled up on the street beside Melissa and me. He told us to get in. Melissa was really scared, and I was pretty worried, too. We drove to the mall and stopped in the empty parking lot. Jesse told us to get out. When he shut the driver's side door, he pulled out his gun.

Melissa started crying, and that made me mad. "Jesse, stop being an asshole. What's the matter, don't you have enough fucking money?"

Jesse grinned. "There's no such thing as enough fucking money."

I knew I should shut up, I was backing him into a corner, but I just couldn't stop myself. "You'd have plenty of fucking money if you didn't smoke up so much. You're stoned on crack all the fucking time. You're cranked right now. You don't know what you're doing, man."

Jesse told me to shut up, then he pointed the gun at Melissa and told her to start walking. I followed them into the trees.

Jesse told Melissa, "It sucks to be you, doesn't it?"

Melissa turned around. "Why?"

Jesse fired, and hit her right in the forehead.

I ran over to Melissa, but she was dead for sure. Behind me, Jesse was going, "Oh fuck, oh fuck." I don't think he meant to fire, because he was freaking out worse than I was.

I turned around and grabbed him by the jacket. "What did you just do? What the fuck did you do?" I don't think he heard me, he just kept standing there looking at Melissa.

I turned around and ran, and I didn't stop till I got home. I started smoking up, and I don't remember the next few days. I don't remember if they found the body or anything, I think that memory may still be blocked. I don't remember if I went to school or talked to anyone, or saw anything about it on the news.

After a week, I had partially buried the memory of Melissa's death, and Jesse and I never mentioned it. But he was going downhill fast. He also had track marks on his arms. He told me that he couldn't find good veins anymore, so he was starting to inject in his penis. I really didn't want to know about that.

And his drug habit was also affecting business. Jesse was shaving the rocks of crack that he was giving me to sell, and my customers thought I was shortchanging them. I finally had to confront him.

I went to his place with Rafe, another dealer buddy that Jesse was messing over, and we confronted him. The problem was that Jesse was high, and Rafe was pretty high too, and the whole thing turned into a shouting match. I pulled my gun on Jesse to make him shut up, then tried to calm Rafe down. But when I turned to Rafe, I squeezed the trigger. I could have killed Jesse, but by sheer dumb luck I just got him in the leg. I kept it cool, like I had meant to do it, but I got out of there fast and ran all the way home.

I looked at myself in the mirror, and I looked like walking death. I was sick of what I had become; it wasn't who I was supposed to be. I thought about how my mother would feel if she saw me now, and it felt worse than dying. I gathered all the drugs I had in the house, took them into the bathroom, and flushed them.

When I put the drugs down the toilet, something seemed to break inside me. It felt like I was turning inside out. And suddenly, I didn't feel angry anymore. I just felt numb. I think that was the moment I blocked all the memories of what Ursula had done to me. Everything was just gone. It would be years before I remembered it all again.

I buried my gun. It was winter, and the ground was frozen; I had to scrape away the dirt with a kitchen knife to get a hole big enough. I buried the gun in one spot, and the clip and bullets in another.

I went back to Jesse and apologized for shooting him. I told him that I wasn't going to deal drugs anymore. I sounded different; I wasn't talking gangsta slang, I was just speaking like a normal guy. I think it spooked him, because he let me walk away without an argument. That was the end of my relationships with my drug buddies. I was out of the brotherhood.

Chapter Sixteen

Uncomfortably Numb

Getting rid of the drug habit wasn't so easy. I was addicted to crack, but not badly; I was dopesick for a couple of weeks, and that was that. Giving up pot was a hundred times harder. I'd been smoking up almost daily since I was twelve, and by now I was sixteen. It had been my only friend through years of hell, and I didn't know how to live without it. And all my friendships were built around pot, and I lost all my friends when I stopped smoking up. I smoked three packs of Export 'A' per day and lived on black coffee, TV, and heavy metal music. It took a year to get myself straight, without any help.

I also missed the money I was making as a dealer. I went from having my own income and buying anything I wanted to stealing from Eddie's wallet for food money. Eddie wasn't home much now, and when he was, he would just bang around and yell and then go sleep it off. I was living on my own, more or less. I preferred it that way, but sometimes I got lonely.

One of the people I stayed friends with was Mark from next door. We'd been hanging out together ever since he moved in, and I'd gotten to know his parents, Dan and Denise. They seemed like an awesome family, and I went over to their apartment a lot. Sometimes when I was over at Mark's place, I fantasized about being part of his family.

Denise was French-Canadian, and spoke some French at home; my own French was still pretty bad, but I could understand her. She was kind of short and chunky with straight black hair, and she was in a wheelchair because of some kind of sickness, but she was very strong-minded and she ran the family. She used to call me "Turkey" as sort of a pet name, and I loved it. Dan was an ex-addict, and he was rail-thin and tattooed. We both liked heavy metal music, and I enjoyed talking to him. Mark was a bit older than I was; he had a job and a steady girlfriend, and he was like a big brother to me. His brother, Mel, was a year or two younger than me, and he was a spoiled brat. He had some kind of mental disability, even though he wasn't in special education. I didn't like him, he was a pain in the ass, but I was nice to him out of politeness.

Denise felt sorry for me, living with Eddie. She told me that she could hear him yelling at me through the walls. She invited me over for meals, which helped when Eddie didn't have anything in his wallet for me to take.

One night, Eddie didn't come home. I didn't miss him, but I was nearly out of food money. He didn't come home the next night either. I didn't know what to do, so I went to Denise. She phoned around to different hospital emergency rooms but couldn't find him.

On the third day, someone from the hospital called. Eddie was drying out in their psychiatric ward. I guess he lost his wallet, and it took a couple of days for him to make enough sense that they knew who to contact. Mark and I went down to see him. He looked okay, and the ward let him go out to lunch with us. He bought us burgers and poutine, and had a few beers with his lunch. He used some breath freshener before going back to the hospital. I thought, "You asshole, you're never going to change." Eddie spent a week in the hospital. When he came home, my grandfather came to Ottawa for a meeting. He had found a program in Mississauga that treated addictions, and he wanted to check Eddie into it. The program would take a few months, and I was supposed to move in with my grandfather; then, when Eddie came out, I would move back in with him.

For the first time, I said no. I didn't want to leave Ottawa. I had built a life here; as shitty as it was, it was mine. I had stayed with my grandfather on summer vacations, and I knew what living with him would be like — I would be treated like a five-year-old. I could take it for two weeks, but three months would drive me crazy. And then living with Eddie again — I knew that the program wouldn't change him. I told my grandfather that I wanted to stay in Ottawa.

Eddie suggested that I move in with Denise. He had already talked to her about it. I nearly fell off the sofa. It was like the answer to a prayer. My grandfather was mad; he said that I was turning my back on my family. And he was right. But the way I saw it, they had turned their backs on me for years. I had the chance for a real family, and I wanted it bad.

So when Eddie went to Mississauga for his treatment program at the end of my school year, I moved in with Dan and Denise. I shared a room with Mel. I started calling Denise "Mom" and Dan "Dad." Mark would introduce me to his friends as his brother, and I became part of the gang. Denise cooked real meals, it was like having a home for the first time since my mom died. But there were a couple of warning signs, if I had been interested in seeing them.

Mark fought with his brother a lot, and got mouthy with his mom and Dan. He kept getting kicked out of the house, and then came back again after a few weeks. Another problem that came up was my money. When I moved out from Eddie, the government started giving me a cheque every month. I didn't know much about it, because Denise handled everything. She said that she was saving the money up for me so I could go to college or if I needed it for something big. Once, I asked her for some of it; she said most of it wasn't there, and she needed to save the rest for me. I didn't understand, and it bothered me, but I didn't press the issue.

We moved to another apartment building at the end of the summer — Dan and Denise moved a lot, I found out — and Denise started to change a bit. She told people that I was a "special child" and that I was manic-depressive. I don't know where she got that idea, and it kind of got on my nerves. Still, it wasn't that big a deal, and besides, I had nowhere else to go.

The new apartment only had two bedrooms, so it was pretty crowded. Judy, Denise's sister-in-law, lived nearby. Her husband was in prison for fraud, so she had room at her place. I moved in with her for about three months, which was okay because she was a really nice lady. She was also gone on weekends visiting her husband, so I had some peace and quiet.

In the meantime, Denise got an apartment in a building that was for people in wheelchairs, still just a two-bedroom place, and she had me move back in with the family. But she stopped treating me like a son. She seemed mad at me all the time and criticized everything I did. Finally, she told me to stop calling her "Mom." By that time, I didn't care. I didn't think of her as a mom anymore. Things always turned to shit in the end.

But I didn't get mad at her, the way I did with Ursula or Eddie. I could feel my anger, but I couldn't bring it to the surface. I was always smiling and apologizing to try to keep

Denise off my back, but I couldn't stand up for myself anymore. I stopped fighting at school and became this quiet, nerdy little kid. At night, I would cry for hours, silently so Denise couldn't hear me.

Denise was always short of money. She made sure I wrote to my relatives a lot; when they sent me money for my birthday or Christmas, she would make me give it to her.

During the winter of grade twelve, Denise started going to a church called the Holy Spirit Tabernacle. Her legs started getting better around that time. She decided that it was a miracle, and she became some kind of super-Christian. She didn't actually change, but every time I did something she didn't like, she would treat it like a sin. When I listened to heavy metal music, or watched action movies, or looked at the Sunshine Girl in the newspaper, she would get in my face with "Do you want *this* or do you want *Jesus*?" She ended up throwing out a lot of my tapes and CDs.

Of course, we all started going to church every Sunday. I hadn't gone to church since my mom died, and I didn't mind the Tabernacle. Some of the people there were really nice, the way you would expect Christians to be. Everybody liked Denise, she was good at fooling people. I felt comfortable praying there, even though it was really different from Catholic mass. I even tried raising my hands when I prayed like everyone else was doing, but Denise got furious; she said I didn't know what it meant and I was making a mockery. Nobody else seemed to mind, but I stopped doing it anyway.

I also went to Bible study group on Wednesday nights. There was this really nice girl there named Alma, and she was the main reason for going, but I also did it to get away from home for a while. It was hard to have friends anywhere else — Denise embarrassed me if I brought any friends home, and she always seemed to be around when I went out anywhere. If I went to a friend's house, she would track me down and phone them, just to keep tabs on me. I finally gave up on having friends.

I graduated high school in June 1999. I was nineteen years old. I was so glad to be done with school, and I felt a real sense of accomplishment for once. Staying in school through all the shit that had happened over the past five years had been nearly impossible, but I had done it. Then Denise opened her mouth and told me that my diploma didn't mean anything, I guess because it was basic level or something.

Aunt Claire and Uncle Pierre came to my graduation ceremony; so did Janice and Eddie. I have photos with them, and with Denise, in my graduation robe and cap. I also kept a photo of me and Mrs. LaSalle. She had been the only one who cared if I stayed in school or not, and I was going to miss her.

After the ceremony, I went back with my aunt and uncle to their trailer in Sudbury. We stopped by my mom's grave in Astorville. I always thought she was buried in North Bay, but this was like a family cemetery, a lot of my relatives from the past hundred years or more are buried there. My uncle took a picture of me by my mom's grave, but it turned out funny. There were a bunch of orange globes all around me in the photo. Anyway, he threw it out.

I spent two weeks at the trailer and got to see my cousins again for the first time in eight years. Then I went to Timmins and spent another two weeks with my Aunt Babette's family. My grandmother looked so much smaller than I remembered that it was kind of a shock; I teased her a bit about how much she had shrunk. It was so great to see my mother's family again, I cried all the way back to Ottawa. I didn't want to go back to Denise.

The next September, I started at a vocational program. After completing the classroom part, we were placed in real jobs. I started working as a dishwasher at a restaurant called Fonzie's. After my co-op, the boss called my teacher, Darla, and said that they wanted to hire me. I was really happy — I loved working there.

Fonzie's was set up like a fifties diner, with booths, a lunch counter, and even a jukebox. All the food was made from scratch, and I helped with food preparation as well as doing dishes. I helped Mustapha, the cook, make the batter for the six-layer chocolate cakes and the stock for the best gravy I have ever tasted before or since. I cut up the potatoes for home fries, and when the cheese grating machine broke down, I used to grate ten-pound blocks of cheese. I loved hanging out with the guys there, and they treated me like an adult. It felt great.

One of the waitresses, Celia, was really hot, even though she was a bit older than me. We both ended up on the night shift, and a lot of times we did the closing together. We started talking, then flirting, and after a while we would make out in her van after our shift. I hadn't had a girlfriend since giving up drugs, and I was really enjoying the relationship with Celia.

Then one evening, when I was working in the kitchen, I noticed Denise and the family out front having dinner. And, oh shit, they were in Celia's section. I saw her talking to them. Denise told her I was mentally retarded or something. That night, Celia broke up with me. Worse yet, she told all the other workers about it, and they all started teasing me. I couldn't take it, and I quit. I had really loved that job.

After quitting Fonzie's, I was really depressed. Denise found a program in the area called the Clubhouse. It was a day program for people with mental problems. I went for two months or so and then quit. The other people there were a lot worse off than I was, and I just didn't want to be there. I wanted to work.

Denise started sending out resumés for me, and I got called in for an interview at a Wendy's near my house. I got the job and started working food prep. I took a bit longer to learn the procedures than other people, but I worked hard and finally learned all the jobs in the kitchen, except sandwich prep (which was usually done by separate staff). I learned to open the restaurant, close it, even take deliveries. I helped make the chili and salads, and I was one of their best fry cooks.

I loved working, because it gave me somewhere to go. My work felt more like home to me, and I became a workaholic. One two-week pay period, I worked eighty-five hours. I would work from six in the morning to ten at night if they needed me. On my days off, I would call in and ask for hours.

But at home, I couldn't do anything right. I smiled till my face hurt and apologized for whatever Denise was complaining about. I would come home from a twelve-hour shift and there would be a sink full of dirty dishes waiting for me. Then she would wake me at eight the next morning to vacuum the house. What really pissed me off was that nobody else in the house was working — and they were home all day.

My paycheque was direct-deposited to my account, but Denise had the only bank card. She gave me an allowance of twenty dollars per week and half a pack of cigarettes per day. Then she started bringing home credit card applications and making me sign them. I never saw the credit cards, and I found out later that she had run up thousands of dollars of debt under my name. I also learned that she was writing my relatives and asking for money.

Denise was becoming a real control freak, to the point where it was getting creepy. She even tried to pressure me into wearing briefs instead of boxer because, as she said, "You don't have enough control over your penis in boxers." She lost that battle, but the whole episode made me nervous.

When I lost my temper or tried to argue, Denise would threaten to tell my father or grandfather. It was always "What would Eddie say about that?" Not that I gave a flying fuck what Eddie said. He was still in Mississauga. He came out to visit every couple of months, but he spent more time talking to Denise than to me.

I didn't see much of Janice, either. She was working at a jewellery store at the mall and going to university. Once I visited her at the mall. She had given me a watch for Christmas, and I was wearing it; it was a really nice watch. She noticed that there was a bit of food caught in the clasp, and it was all "Ohhhh, Chris!" My stepsister Jacinta was in the store too, so I figured that the five-minute lecture I got was for her benefit. I never wore the watch after that, it just wasn't worth the aggravation.

At work, I felt like I belonged. My boss, Angus, told me I was the best employee he had. I even made Employee of the Month, and my biggest ambition was to be Employee of the Year. I think I would have made it, too, if Denise hadn't dragged me off to Kingston.

It wasn't all work at Wendy's: we got a little crazy sometimes. After the restaurant closed, we had ketchup fights in the kitchen. The place looked like a crime scene by the time we were done, but we always cleaned up before we left. Another time, one of the managers had an entire canister of Coke syrup explode on him. He was sticking to the floor when he walked, and he looked like the Swamp Creature; he was furious, but we couldn't help laughing after he went home to shower and change.

Mark moved home again while I was working at Wendy's, and he had a really nice girlfriend named Sylvie. They got jobs at my Wendy's, and we all worked together for three months. That was the best. Mark and Sylvie were saving up to get a place together, and they asked if I wanted to move in with them and share the rent. I nearly had a heart attack when they asked, and I couldn't wait to get the hell away from Denise. Then Mark and Sylvie broke up, and that was the end of that. Mark got kicked out of the house for hitting his mom soon after the breakup. I can't agree with hitting any woman, but I have to admit that I wasn't sorry for Denise at all.

But losing the chance to move out of that hellhole was more than I could take. I broke down at work one day, and Angus asked me what was wrong. He told me that he was more than my boss, he was my friend. So I told him about Denise and how trapped I felt; he was really angry about Denise keeping my money and about the way I was being treated. A few weeks later, he called me into the office for a talk. He had just broken up with his girlfriend, and he had a spare room in his house that he would be willing to rent to me. I was even more excited about this than I had been about moving in with Mark and Sylvie.

A couple of weeks later, Denise asked Angus to come over to the house for a talk. I was shitting bricks worrying about how she might mess up my chance of moving out. Sure enough, she asked Angus to see if I could get transferred to another Wendy's — in Kingston! I couldn't believe that she would actually move to another city two hours away just to keep me from moving out. There were probably other reasons, but that didn't make me feel any better.

It hurt so bad to say goodbye to all the staff at Wendy's; Angus even cried a bit. I was angrier than I had been in years. I was feeling like committing suicide or murdering Denise, one or the other.

The new Wendy's in Kingston wasn't the same as the one in Ottawa: the managers weren't friendly, and the workers didn't stay for very long. I didn't have any problem with the work — I could have done it in my sleep — but I didn't like it anymore.

And Denise was still on her super-Christian kick, so there was religious music on in the house day and night. Almost every word out of her mouth was a complaint about me. I tried to put up with it, but every day on my way home from work I thought of just running away and camping out in the park. I was stuck, though: she still had my bank card.

Finally, Denise let me look for another place to live. We checked out several boarding houses, and I liked this old three-storey house about ten minutes away from my work. I moved in as fast as I could. It wasn't a great place, but anything was better than the hellhole I was stuck in with Denise.

The boarding house used to be a three-family home; each floor was like an apartment, with three or four people on each level. I was on the third floor: the living room on that level had been divided into two bedrooms, and one was mine. I shared the bathroom with two roommates, and the kitchen was our smoking area, since we all had meals in the kitchen on the first floor. Our landlady, Nella, was from Nigeria; she did all the cooking and cleaning for us. I remember Denise trying to tell her that I was "special" and couldn't look out for myself, but Nella didn't believe her. She always treated me like an adult.

My roommates were pretty weird, to tell the truth, but we got along okay. Algie was older than me; he was schizophrenic and he always thought that people were fucking with his head. I could kind of relate to that. Zane was really old and just didn't have anywhere else to go. He just sat around smoking and watching TV all day. The other guys who lived there were kind of bums and winos, but I wasn't scared. I knew how to fight, but nobody bothered me. It was actually pretty peaceful.

Not that Denise gave up on controlling me — hell no. She dropped by whenever she felt like it, and I would have to go over and have supper with them every few days just to shut her mouth. She still had my bank card, and sometimes I had a hard time paying Nella the rent. I still wasn't good at math, but I was pretty sure that money was going missing. I tried to get a new card, and I was issued a temporary one — but the permanent one went to my old place, and I never saw it.

My sister Janice came to see my new place a few times. She would go through my stuff every time she came over, and I hated it — she never even asked. Janice didn't like the place, but I didn't care, I wasn't moving back with Denise no matter what.

It was a good thing, in a way, that I had moved in when I did. One of the other residents was a woman named Helen who was really depressed. I used to talk to her and try to cheer her up, and she was a really sweet person. She had scars all over her arms and legs from cutting herself; it was creepy to look at them and think that she could do that to herself. One night, I heard crying downstairs and went to see what was going on. Helen had cut herself all over with a piece of sawblade. The place was a total bloody mess, the sofa was soaked with blood so dark it looked black. Helen was still cutting herself and crying, and there were cuts all over her arms and legs. I told her to stop, I cared about her, and, eventually, she gave me the sawblade. Then I called the police, and stayed with her till the ambulance came. I spent a couple of hours cleaning up the blood in the living room. I soaked three big bath towels so bloody that I had to throw them out. There was still a big dark spot on the carpet, and the foam in the sofa was still sticky, but it was the best I could do. When Nella came in the next morning, I told her what had happened, and she thanked me for cleaning it up. She had already been to see Helen, who had nearly died from blood loss and was covered with stitches. Still, she was alive. Helen never came back to the boarding house; but Nella told me that Helen had talked to the police and had laid charges against a priest who had been a friend of her family and who had molested her as a child.

After I had been in my new place about three or four months, I went with Janice and her boyfriend to visit my dad's sister, Aunt Olga, in Mississauga. This was in July of 2001. Aunt Olga asked me if I would like to move in with her family. I was thrilled at the idea of getting out of Kingston and away from Denise forever. I also wanted to have a family again, and I had always gotten along with my aunt and uncle and cousins when I was a kid. I didn't find out until later that her real plan was to get me into a group home for mentally disabled people.

I went back in August to set up some things for the move. One was the application to George Brown College's vocational program. The other was a meeting with my new social worker, Mary. I was really looking forward to my new life. When I went back to the boarding house, I didn't tell Denise a thing: I was sure she'd do something to ruin it. I got some boxes from work and started packing. My aunt drove up the next day and picked me up. My troubles were over; I was back with my family again.

PART III

MARY

Repeatedly in the testimony of survivors there comes a moment when a sense of connection is restored by another person's unaffected display of generosity. Something [...] that the victim believes to be irretrievably destroyed — faith, decency, courage — is reawakened by an example of common altruism.

—Judith Lewis Herman

Chapter Seventeen

The Graveyard of Memories

I got Chris home from Tim Hortons; he was oriented enough to go downstairs by himself while I ran for the Ativan. This time, he didn't have to go into a trance in order to remember.

"I was asleep in my bedroom in the house in Ottawa. Ursula shook me awake, I didn't know why she was there. She was naked and had a knife in her hand. She stuck it under my chin. She said, 'I'm not playing around anymore. I want you to fuck me hard.'

"I jumped out of the bed and ran to the door. It was shut, and it was late at night, everybody was asleep. I pissed myself all over my pajamas. I couldn't move, it was like I was frozen to the spot. I was saying, 'What are you talking about? I don't understand,' and I started crying.

"Ursula came over to me and told me to shut the fuck up. She dragged me back to the bed and made me take off my pajamas and lie down. She had handcuffs and she made me put my arms up and shackled me to the top of the bed. Then she got on top of me, she had the knife at my throat and I was still crying. She put me inside her, and started moving and saying stuff to me. Finally she got off me, and took off the handcuffs. She told me that she would kill me if I told anyone. Then she left and shut the door behind her. I just lay there, I couldn't move, I was just shaking all over."

Chris and I were both drained after this episode, so we just sat on the bed in silence for a few minutes. He had a look of relief, the kind you get when you finally throw up after hours of feeling deathly nauseous. I didn't want to stir things up any further that night, but I was confused about Chris's rantings on the trip home.

"Chris, what were you talking about in the car? You were saying something about a coffin coming out of the grave and opening up. Can you remember?"

He frowned, trying to switch gears in his head. "I have a graveyard in my mind," he said. "A place I buried memories when they were … too bad to think about. This time, I could see a grave opening up, all the dirt just exploding out of the hole, and then the coffin rose up beside the headstone … and opened … and something came out, kind of like a mist or fog. And then I remembered about Ursula."

"You mean you actually buried your memories? In coffins, in a graveyard, with headstones and everything?"

"Yeah, well, I forgot what was in the graves until tonight. But the graveyard's been there for a long time. When I was little, it used to be a meadow where I could go and play and nothing bad ever happened. Part of me would be in class or in my house, but part of me would be there. It was just as real as the real world, and sometimes I liked it a whole lot better. Then when I got older, I made it into a graveyard. I put iron fences up and an iron gate so the memories couldn't escape. There was a door at the far end where the memory would be pulled in. A new memory just looked like a black blob. Then I would build a coffin in the workshop just outside the gate;

it had all my woodworking tools. I would carve a grave marker out of stone. Then I'd get my tractor from the caretaker's shed, and drive into the graveyard and dig the grave. The memory would kind of wander around while I was doing this, but it couldn't get out of the graveyard. Then I'd get my tractor, and load the coffin on the trailer, and haul it over by the grave. I'd catch the memory and wrestle it into the coffin. I'd nail the coffin lid shut, I had a toolbox with me, then I'd hoist the coffin into the grave and shovel the dirt back in. After that, I'd haul the grave marker in and set it up, and that would be it."

"You actually did all this in your head?"

"Oh, yeah. I have to do maintenance on my machinery, and I have to cut the grass in the graveyard and everything. There's a ride-on mower in the shed. It's a big graveyard."

I knew I was going to regret it, but I asked anyway. "How many graves are there?"

"Hundreds. It's a really big graveyard."

Oh, shit.

CHAPTER EIGHTEEN

PTSD 101

I had figured that, once Chris recovered the sexual abuse memory, the worst would be over and he would start to recover. Instead, as he continued to remember more incidents, he got sicker and sicker.

The vomiting got so bad that his medication didn't have time to get into his system before being thrown up. I gave him Gatorade to try to keep him hydrated and Ensure to get some nourishment into him. He was downing Ativan like Tic Tacs, and he still had anxiety attacks and drop seizures constantly. When he slept, the nightmares were horrific; when he was awake, the memories were almost as bad.

To explain one memory, Chris asked me for a cardboard tube from a paper towel roll. "Okay, now I need to use a doorway." He opened his bedroom door as wide as it could go and stuffed the tube into the door jamb, in the space between the top and bottom hinges. He was like a kid setting up a science experiment. Once he had everything in place, Chris turned to me.

"Ursula used to make me put my penis in the door like this. Then she would shut the door until it latched." He shut the bedroom door, squashing the cardboard tube flat.

I just stood there. Part of my mind was trying to figure out if it was physically possible to flatten a penis that much. It wasn't one of those things that came up in biology class. The other part of my mind was wondering how Chris could explain this so calmly.

"How could you stand it?"

"Well, Ursula would be behind me, pushing on me to hold me there. She would keep opening and shutting the door until I blacked out."

"Why couldn't you run away from her?"

"Oh, Ursula used to wait until everyone was gone, then she would make me strip naked and put handcuffs and shackles on my ankles. It was really hard to go downstairs, the chains on the shackles were too short and I had to sort of hop. I was always worried that I'd trip, because I wouldn't be able to break my fall." Chris had pulled the cardboard roll out of the doorway and was casually examining it. "She used to make me follow her around the house while she looked for things to hit me with. She smashed the toaster down on my penis once. It broke the toaster and she had to get a new one." He smirked at the memory, as if he had gotten back at her that time.

Once again, I walked away feeling that I had just passed the signpost to the Twilight Zone. How in hell could Chris be so calm about these horrific memories, and yet get so furious at Dan and Denise? Could it be that the memories weren't real? But if they weren't, how were they making him so sick? And where would he get these weird details? The stories he told were so far beyond anything I had read about in abuse literature — and, to be honest, anything I could picture happening — that I couldn't take it in; and Chris's greatest fear was of not being believed.

No one seemed to have any answers — not the doctors, or the psychiatric clinic staff, or Chris's psychiatrist, or even the neurologist who had been called in. I decided that it was time to take things into my own hands. It was time to pull out my secret weapon, the one resource that had never failed me.

My library card.

As a card-carrying geek since childhood, I loved the vast ocean of information that was contained in the rows upon rows of books in a public library. Research came as naturally to me as swimming does to a seal. During my years at the agency, one of my projects was a collaboration between social services organizations and the public library to build a collection of disability-related materials; I knew the system inside out. If there was any information on post-traumatic stress disorder in the Peel Library, I was going to find it.

The Central Library was modern architecture done right: it was five levels of rings around a central well of light, pouring from the glass ceiling to the courtyard on the lowest level. It was calm and spacious and sane, everything I needed after the three months at home. The afternoon spent teasing titles out of the computer system and tracking library numbers up and down the stacks was as relaxing as a day at the spa. I bagged about half a dozen volumes and headed home in a golden haze of confidence. Surely the answers we needed were somewhere in these books.

They were, and they weren't. The basic facts about post-traumatic stress disorder were covered in several of the volumes that did explain a lot of Chris's behaviour. PTSD is considered a type of anxiety disorder, caused by exposure to traumatic events such as death, injury, or other terrifying experiences. The experience causes a response of extreme fear or horror and makes the person feel helpless to protect themselves. Unlike other mental disorders, post-traumatic stress disorder can happen to anyone; it is the response that a normal mind makes to an abnormal situation.

I picture PTSD this way: a person has a lifelong experience of the way life is — what is and isn't possible, what can happen and what you can do about it. Then an event comes along that fries this reality, like a celluloid frame melting in a movie projector. It's not just a bad experience — it's an experience that rewrites the concept of bad. It's the moment in the nightmare that scares you awake; it's the scene in the horror movie makes you cover your eyes and scrunch in your seat. It's that moment translated into real life. And, just like getting shot in real life is different from what we see on TV, real horror causes real damage that can take months, years, even a lifetime to repair.

Then the event is over, and normal life resumes. The problem is that you now have two versions of reality, and they contradict each other. The safe, controllable reality is not solid anymore; it is a rind of rotting ice over freezing black water. Your mind has to find ways not to break through the ice.

The mind's strategy is to reinforce the safe version of reality by denying that the traumatic version even exists. The ultimate example of this is actually burying the memory, as Chris did. Some people just block out parts of the experience. Others avoid remembering; they don't talk about it or even think about it. They "get over it." In order to do this, they have to stay away from people, places, or activities that may remind them of the trauma, since these now become "triggers" for involuntary memories.

The problem with this solution is that the fear, pain, and shame connected with the trauma also have to be buried; and in order to numb those feelings, the mind has to numb all its other feelings as well. It's like a shot of novocaine to the emotions. The person loses interest in their favourite activities, feels detached from friends or family, and just doesn't care about anything. I remembered Chris's Eeyore expression those first few months; he could have been the poster child for emotional numbing.

While the mind is busy forgetting about the traumatic experience, the nervous system is still reacting to it. Inside the head of a PTSD victim is a tiny war room on DEFCON 2, alert to every sight and sound in a world that has now become unpredictable, uncontrollable, and terrifying. Adrenaline levels skyrocket easily, and stay high longer than in a normal person. Cortisol, another stress-related hormone, increases and causes physiological changes. The person becomes irritable, bothered by every noise or disturbance, and easily startled; they have trouble relaxing, concentrating, or sleeping.

This cluster of symptoms was totally Chris, who couldn't fall asleep at night and made up for it with quick catnaps throughout the day, who couldn't concentrate enough to watch a movie all the way through and would replay his videotapes over and over until they actually wore out, who had a startle response that reminded me of Sylvester the Cat in the cartoons: if you came up behind him unexpectedly, you would have to peel him off the ceiling.

Another symptom I saw in Chris was hypervigilance. He never really relaxed; he was constantly alert and hyper-aware of everything around him. Once, just before Christmas, Chris and I were leaving the house, when he paused in the doorway. "That red Saturn looks like my dad's car." I looked around and couldn't see anything, until he pointed out a small red car almost a block away, half-hidden in a row of four or five parked cars. I was shocked when we drove by the car and saw Eddie in the driver's seat; he was staking out my house just the way he had watched Barbara's house. He looked just as shocked that we had caught him, and the car was gone when we got back. But I couldn't get over the fact that Chris had seen and recognized the car, fifty yards away, in a split second.

Other symptoms involved the memories themselves, which don't go away just because they are being ignored. They're like balloons being pushed underwater: it takes a lot of effort and energy to hold them down, and they still keep popping up somehow. The books had descriptions of the ways that traumatic memories can surface, and Chris had already experienced some of them. The nightmares about Zombie Mom; the recurrent rages at Dan and Denise that obsessed him for months; and, the most frightening type so far, the full-on flashback, when Chris had seemed trapped in the memory as if it were a time warp. Even the physiological symptoms like the pseudoseizures, vomiting, and "out-of-body" episodes were probably related to traumatic memories.

I began to see why Chris had looked as if he had an intellectual disability. If you think of mental energy as a bank account, he was drowning in debt. He was spending all his energy damming up terrible events from his past and trying to protect himself from dangers in the present. There was nothing left over to use for learning, or working, or even relaxing and enjoying himself. No wonder he crashed and burned; his nervous breakdown was his brain's way of declaring bankruptcy.

The books also contained recommendations for treating post-traumatic stress disorder, and this was good news and bad news. Chris had to do the one thing he feared even more than dying: he had to remember.

As long as the memories were being pushed away from consciousness, they pushed back; and that was the engine that drove the symptomatology of post-traumatic stress disorder. It was like having shrapnel in a wound that had scabbed over; the wound would keep re-infecting and wouldn't heal until the object causing the damage was removed. The treatment for PTSD was to allow the memories to surface, talk them out, "process" them, and find a way to reconcile them with the non-traumatic version of reality. This was easier said than done: as we were finding out, a traumatic memory can be just as terrifying as the event that caused it. It was a cruel paradox that Chris had to relive the horrors of his abuse in order to heal from them.

I wondered if there was a way to send his abusers to Hell twice; it seemed only fair.

Two things bothered me about all the books I had read so far. First, I couldn't get an idea about what the recovery process for PTSD was like. You had a trauma, you got sick, you talked it out, you got well. A cancer patient would be given an idea of what to expect from the illness, from the treatment, from recovery, and would know how long it would take to get well. I was desperate for an idea of what Chris could expect, and what we could do about it. I was afraid — the thought startled me as it surfaced — that Chris was going to die if I couldn't find out how to help him.

The second problem was the variety of traumas described in the books. They ranged from car wrecks to kidnappings, from a single rape to a childhood incinerated by abuse. The authors seemed to use these examples interchangeably, as if they were all the same sort of experience. In a sense, they were: in the sense that a broken leg is the same sort of injury as an accident that leaves you in traction. It's just common sense that different levels of the same injury cause different levels of damage, and Chris seemed much sicker than any of the people described in the books. Every time we talked through a memory, he'd come up with another one. It just seemed to make him worse. The idea of talking him through his PTSD sounded good on paper, but I felt like I was being handed a bottle of aspirin to treat a sucking chest wound.

The strategy that had worked best for the last three months was simply to follow Chris's lead. He had a superhuman capacity for survival, and maybe we both needed to trust his instincts until something else came along. He needed a lot of physical contact: I would hug him fifty times a day. He needed to talk: I sat and listened by the hour. He needed reassurance; I would tell him how much I loved and admired him, and how incredibly brave and good he was. He needed to feel safe and loved and believed; as long as he had that, he seemed to have an underlying confidence in himself. Living things are healed by God and themselves, and sometimes it's best to put them in a nice pot on the windowsill, water them when they need it, and trust them for the rest.

CHAPTER NINETEEN

PETS ALLOWED

In February of 2002, my grandson Connor decided to throw Chris a surprise birthday party. Connor was three years old, so he decided on a Spider-Man birthday cake, balloons, and streamers, hung up with masking tape because that was all we could find. I found a banner saying "BONNE FÊTE" (Chris later explained that it is not pronounced "boney feet"). We set it up in the downstairs kitchen while Chris lurked around the rest of the apartment pretending to be oblivious. When we were ready, Chris came in looking surprised (his version of surprised anyway, which looked as deadpan as any of his other facial expressions, but he did try). We sang "Happy Birthday," and Chris blew out the candles; then he relit them because Connor wanted a turn. We ate birthday cake with inedible red icing and large, chewy blobs of candle wax. Connor gave Chris a present from the dollar store and a card he had made himself, of people who looked like water bugs: the big one was Chris and the little one was him. Chris told me that this had been his first birthday party since his mother died. He didn't say much else about it, but the "BONNE FÊTE" banner was up on the kitchen wall for months.

Chris had the basement to himself since Dana had moved in with her boyfriend. He had taken over the family room, with the fireplace and built-in bookcase. It was homier than the spare room, but still pretty empty after he had spread out his few possessions. It was also pretty isolated; I was worried about him being down there by himself, especially at night. After talking it over with my husband, I asked Chris if he would like a pet to keep him company.

"You really mean it? You would really let me have one?"

"Would you want to get a kitten? They aren't much work, and Nika's used to cats. I used to have one." Our husky, Nika, used to follow our cranky old tomcat around for hours, with her nose practically up the cat's butt. When the cat would turn around, Nika would look away innocently; when the cat walked away again, Nika went right back into stalking mode. She loved that cat, but she nearly gave him a nervous breakdown. But I didn't think Chris needed those details right then.

Chris was deep in thought. "If it's okay with you, I'd like to get a dog. I always wanted a dog, but my mom was allergic. All she let me have was goldfish."

"I'm game, but a dog is a lot more work. Are you sure you're up for it?"

Chris nodded furiously. "Absolutely I can do it! But you're serious? You really mean that I can have a dog?"

And thus began one of the most nerve-wracking weeks of my life. Every fifteen minutes — you could time it by the clock — Chris would thank me for getting him a dog. And ask me when we could get the dog. And ask me again if I still meant it. And apologize for bugging me about it. And thank me again for getting him a dog…

We tried the local Humane Society, but the dogs were all with foster families. So we made the rounds of the local pet shops, and I couldn't believe the prices — and we didn't even need a purebred, just a nice little mutt. And we needed one soon, or Chris was going to explode. Looking forward to something was an excruciating ordeal for him; in the back of his mind, he was preparing for me to change my mind. Until we actually got the puppy, he wasn't sure that it would really happen, no matter how many times I tried to reassure him.

Finally, I noticed a small pet shop in a mall about two blocks from our house. We checked it out, and Chris fell in love with a nondescript brindled bundle of energy that he named Hazzard. (Chris had been fanatical about *The Dukes of Hazzard* ever since he was eight years old; he had developed his very first crush on Daisy Duke.) I put a down payment on Hazzard and planned to pick him up the next day.

That night, Chris started having a new symptom. I first noticed it when he was watching TV. His gaze drifted upward every few minutes; then he would shake his head and refocus on the television. Later, when he talked to me, he looked at my forehead instead of looking me in the eye. Finally, when he couldn't look down at his plate to eat supper, I had to ask if something was wrong.

"Well, yeah, it's something I used to do when I was in my teens. My eyes would just roll all the way up and stay there. When it was really bad, they stayed like that for hours; it was hard to get around because you can't see where you're going."

"Does it hurt?"

"Not this time, but sometimes I would get muscle spasms in my neck too, and it would pull my head way back.

Once, I was bending backward so hard I couldn't stand up. That hurt really bad."

"Didn't you go to the doctor?"

"No, Ursula just told everybody I was doing it for attention."

By this time, Chris was literally facing the ceiling; he would try to force his head down, but as soon as he relaxed his muscles, it swung smoothly upward as if there were hydraulics in his neck. His eyes weren't rolled all the way back in his head, as in a seizure; they were just looking up, as if he were stargazing right through the roof.

I was seeing another emergency room visit in our stars, but I tried something else first. I called Telehealth Ontario and was connected to a public health nurse. She actually had an idea about what was happening: it seemed to be a kind of neuromuscular dystonia induced by stress. She suggested trying a cough suppressant with dextromethorphan in it, to block the nerve signals to the muscles; if that didn't work, it would be another trip to the hospital for Chris. I had some Children's Benadryl left over from Connor's last cold; Chris downed half the bottle and slept for about fourteen hours.

Either the sleep or the medicine had done the trick, because he woke up with no problems — until I mentioned picking Hazzard up that afternoon. Chris spent the day studying the light fixtures until I packed him up in the car, dystonia and all, and went to get the new puppy. He held onto my arm as I guided him through the pet shop aisle to Hazzard's pen. The store owner handed the puppy over with some misgivings, but Chris cuddled his new baby with a beatific smile on his face, and his eyes on the pet shop ceiling, while we finished the paperwork for the sale.

Once we got Hazzard home, I set up the spare room downstairs with food, water, and some newspaper. The dystonia was as bad as the day before, but Chris couldn't have cared less; he and Hazzard were exploring the basement together, and whatever one left standing, the other knocked over. The puppy was about eight weeks old: short-haired, long-eared, all legs and tail, full of energy, with a deep, baying bark that shook the windows and made the door chimes ring. He was teething, and he chewed or tugged on everything he could get his mouth around. Chris was besotted with him; for the first time, I could see the PTSD lifting and the real boy underneath, the one that could have been if the abuse hadn't happened. It was wonderful, and heartbreaking.

Of course, Hazzard slept in Chris's bed that night. Chris stayed up all night just stroking him and watching him snore. The dystonia faded significantly by the next day, although it kept coming back for almost a week. We found that the best treatment was sleep; when Chris woke up, his eyes were usually under control again.

Like many growing boys, Hazzard looked like he was put together from leftover parts and running on a twelve-volt battery plugged into a six-volt system. He had a mouthful of teeth that reminded me of the cartoon dog in the movie *The Mask*. He chewed everything. He actually ate the floor in Chris's room. It was no-wax linoleum that my husband had installed a couple of years earlier, and it had one teeny rip under the bed. By the time Hazzard finished teething, he had chewed up about a third of it. We didn't find many linoleum scraps, either.

But we bought area rugs and learned to live with it. Hazzard was the light of Chris's life, and he was doing more good than all the meds in the world. He kept Chris focused on something that made him happy, which was a powerful antidote to the memories. He slept at the foot of Chris's bed and would wake him up from nightmares by licking his face, and cuddle with him to calm him down. But I didn't understand how important Hazzard had become until Chris explained more about his internal world.

We were walking Nika and Hazzard in the field behind my house, when Chris casually mentioned that he was moving out of his apartment. I stopped in my tracks.

"What are you talking about? I thought you had decided to live with us. I mean, you can move if you want to, but you should wait for the agency to find a place for you..."

But Chris was horrified by my suggestion that he leave his home with us; he had been talking about the apartment inside his head, which had been his "home away from home" for years.

While the dogs chased each other through the snowbanks and bushes, Chris and I sat down on a log, backed up our conversation, and tried to make sense of Chris's planned "moving-out."

"I have an apartment inside my head, where I really live. Have you seen that video on the music channel, where this really tiny guy is inside the real guy's head, like in a control room, and he pushes buttons and steers the real guy like a machine?"

I nodded. It was a video by the Crash Test Dummies, one of my favourite groups.

"I can do that. It's like what's going on out in the world has nothing to do with me, like my body is something I'm driving. The real me is just looking out through the windshield at everything. So when I get bored, I put my body on automatic pilot and go downstairs to my apartment. It's all furnished, and has a TV and VCR and a Sega system, and I can just hang out and do whatever I want. All the furniture is fastened to the floor so it doesn't slide around when my body is moving. There's a kitchen where I can make meals for myself, and the plates and stuff are magnetized so they stay on the table."

"Good idea. You wouldn't want to make a mess. How did you think of all this?"

"Everything works just like in the real world. I have to clean the apartment and wash the dishes, and I do maintenance on the machinery in the control room. It's my own place, and I don't let anyone else in. I have a lobby, and if someone wants to talk to me he has to buzz my apartment. I can go down, or we can talk on the intercom." Chris was quiet for a minute; then he looked at me with his peculiar, intense gaze. "Lately, I've been letting you and Connor into the apartment for really short visits. You're the first ones. And now I've started packing up some of my stuff, and I'm thinking about moving out. Now that I have a place here, I don't need it as much. And it's there if I ever want to use it."

"Or you might think about subletting it, make a little extra money. There's an apartment shortage in Toronto, you know."

Chris grinned. "I never thought of that. I could walk around with a little sticky note on my forehead saying, 'Apartment for Rent.'"

"You'd have to — I don't know how we could list it." I was impressed: Chris was making an art form out of dissociative disorder. He wasn't psychotic, though; he was aware that his internal world was not part of the reality that he shared with other people. His ability to joke about it was a demonstration of that; a sense of humour requires contact with reality, even if you're just giving it the finger. Psychotic people don't laugh at their delusions.

"So do you let Hazzard in the apartment, or don't you allow pets?"

Chris suddenly turned serious. "Hazzard has been in the apartment ever since I got him. I moved him in there with me right away," he said. "He's a dog. I can trust him. He loves me, and he isn't going to fuck me over. There's nothing to worry about, like there is with people."

Six months later, we both had reason to remember that statement. Even a dog can break your heart.

CHAPTER TWENTY

THE SEVENTH LEVEL OF HELL; OR, DANTE WAS AN OPTIMIST

Back in October, when Chris was having his first nightmares, a male apparition had begun to show up. We didn't pay much attention to "It" (our name for the figure), as we assumed it represented Eddie. We were wrong.

Chris was remembering more about his life after Eddie had moved out. Ursula still took care of Chris and Janice, as well as her own two teenagers. It would have been termed a "blended" family; in reality, it was a malevolent hybrid that sucked Janice in, spat Eddie out, and kept Chris imprisoned and isolated like a fly in a web. Now he began to remember the spider.

After Eddie was removed from the home, Ursula introduced her boyfriend Jacques to the family. Jacques was a big, burly ex-cop who now ran his own car-repair business and body shop out of his garage. He was confident, outgoing, and affable — the polar opposite of Eddie. The four children took to him right away, especially Chris who was desperately hoping for help with the Ursula situation.

"I remember the first time I tried to talk to him about it. I knew he had been a cop, and I figured he would have to help me. He came in wearing a suit, I guess he was going to take

Ursula out that evening. I asked him if I could talk to him in the living room, so he came in and sat on the sofa and looked real serious. I told him that Ursula was sexually abusing me, it was so hard to say it, and then he grinned and said, "I know all about it." I was really confused, and then he leaned forward and said, "Ursula tells me you like it up the ass. Why do you think I'm here?" Then he got up and left, and I could hear him and Ursula laughing as they went out to his car. I went upstairs and threw up for about an hour.

"Not too long after that, Ursula came into my bedroom around midnight, after everyone was asleep. She had a small pistol this time, I'd never seen it before, and she told me to go downstairs with her. We went to the basement, and Jacques was waiting down there for us. He was naked; he was really big and muscular, but he had a fat gut that stuck out like he was pregnant or something. He took the pistol from Ursula, and he pointed it at me and told me not to move. Then they tore my pajamas off me, and Ursula took off her nightgown. Jacques and Ursula had sex on the basement floor while I stood there. Then Jacques got up and came over to me. He had the pistol in his hand.

"He said, 'Get down on your hands and knees.' I couldn't do it, it was like my muscles were frozen. Then he stuck the gun in my face. I could hear him cock it, it sounded really loud, and then it was like my body moved without me even telling it to. I got down on the ground, and Jacques got down on his knees behind me. He wrapped his arms around me and stuck the gun in my mouth. I could feel him shoving and grunting behind me, and it hurt, but I was more scared that he would get too excited and pull the trigger. My legs were numb and it was hard to stay kneeling, but I held still until he was finished."

The Ursula memories were a crack in the dam; the Jacques memories became a deluge. Every night, Chris relived rape sessions that became more and more violent.

Every night, I listened to recollections that I could hardly believe. In the back of my mind, I was frantically hoping that Chris had been hallucinating or dreaming, anything to keep me from facing these horrors as things that really happened to a real person. The experience was unexpectedly isolating for me: I desperately wished that there was someone I could ask about this, or even tell it to, just to hear it out in the open. I started having my own nightmares as my brain kept sloshing over from a deluge of vicarious traumatization. I hadn't yet learned about secondary trauma (also called caregiver trauma), but I was developing a whopping case of it anyway.

Chris began having full flashbacks on a daily basis, which restricted his life severely. He couldn't go out of the house for more than an hour or so without starting a flashback. I worried about him taking the dog for walks by himself, as he could fall over in the middle of a field and lie there for an hour or more. Hazzard became Chris's rescuer when the flashbacks happened, nudging him and licking his face until he came around. But when Chris blanked out while crossing a street and was nearly hit by a bus before he could move again, we realized that he couldn't go out of the house alone.

Chris was also dissociating, or "pulling out of his body," almost constantly. I would notice him sitting quietly with his eyes closed or unfocused and recognize that he was "out." The dissociation was different from flashbacks — Chris was aware of everything going on around him, and could bring himself back whenever he wanted. It was a response to stress that he had developed during the rapes; he had been able to "leave" his body and watch from a distance, or even leave the room and go elsewhere until the rape and torture was over.

For Chris, this was a very real experience; he described it as being "cold and a bit creepy," but disconnected from the pain and fear of the assault. Interestingly, the sensations Chris described were similar to those mentioned in astral travel and near-death out-of-body experiences.

The most confusing part of Chris's recollections was the detached, almost bemused attitude he had when describing them. He should have been freaking out; I certainly was. But he would talk about the tile patterns he remembered on the floor in one breath and being slit with razor blades and doused with alcohol in the next — "or concentrated lemon juice, that's worse actually, because the alcohol evaporates but the juice doesn't."

I discovered the answer, finally, in Trauma and Recovery by Dr. Judith Herman. This book became my survival guide, mainly because Dr. Herman was one of the first to discuss extreme PTSD as a different process from "normal" PTSD. She also described several of the peculiar symptoms that Chris was having that weren't covered in any of the other resources I had found. For instance, his tendency to remember events in excruciating detail while not being sure what age he was when they happened was typical of traumatic memories: more primitive, sensory memories are sharpened by the traumatic memory process, while the more sophisticated function of longitudinal (timeline) memory is short-circuited.

Trauma also affects memory by "splitting" the components of the memory: what happened, how you felt (both emotionally and physically), and what response you had. Usually, these components are all integrated parts of a whole memory, but traumatic memories may only access one of the parts. When Chris talked about his memories unemotionally, he was remembering the content of his experiences, but the other parts weren't there yet. His dissociative episodes (pulling out of his body) were a behavioural component of his memories; that was what he did when things had happened to him. His panic attacks were affective memories. The full package was the flashback, which completely recreated the event in Chris's mind and body.

I was treated to a full-on behavioural flashback when Chris started vomiting blood one evening. Another immediate trip to the emergency room. Chris was always perfectly calm during these visits, which were becoming routine. This time was very different. He was fine until the doctor put a nasogastric tube down his throat to check the amount of blood in his stomach. Chris became irritable, then angry, even swearing: "I'm not fucking staying here! I want something to eat! I want to fucking smoke!" I had never seen Chris so out of control before, and I had no idea why it was happening. The tube was unpleasant, but it didn't seem to be the reason. After an hour, the doctor determined that the gastric bleeding had stopped; Chris had probably just popped a blood vessel during one of his vomiting sessions. He sent Chris home, and I was embarrassingly aware that the nurses were probably glad to see him go.

As we went back to the car, I asked Chris what was wrong. "When they poked the back of my throat, I thought, 'This feels familiar.' Then I just became enraged. Now I remember why: Jacques and Ursula used to try stuff like that. They actually had a plastic tube shoved up one nostril and pulled out the other. Then they yanked on it till my nose was bleeding; I thought they were going to rip my nose off my face."

Chris was reacting the way he had during the rape sessions. He'd yell at Jacques and Ursula, and they'd just laugh at him. "They liked it when I got mad. When I was in the hospital just now, I didn't know why I was behaving that way, either. I just couldn't stop myself."

As well as the information I was able to get from Dr. Herman's book, I also got some heartening advice. People recovering from extreme PTSD need two things to recover. First and foremost, they need a safe environment, one where they can let down their guard and remember the trauma. Second, they need to experience control over their own lives, to have their needs and decisions respected. (I would have added one thing to the list: credibility. Chris had an absolute need to know he was going to be believed before he opened up.) By sheer luck and instinct, we had been doing things right so far. But I felt that we were going to need more than books to get through this.

CHAPTER TWENTY-ONE

THE HEAD VAMPIRE

By this time, I had been beating the bushes for any kind of resources to help Chris. The only therapy he'd been getting were our nightly conversations and the weekly visits with the psychiatrist to monitor his symptoms and medication. And I was beginning to realize that Dr. Vindar was as confused as I was. Psychiatric training seems to focus on mood disorders like depression, anxiety, and schizophrenia. Nobody had any experience treating PTSD; and nobody wanted to accidentally develop any experience, and start getting PTSD case referrals. It was just like getting psychiatric help for one of my agency clients — no psychiatrist wanted developmentally disabled people for patients, either.

I made the rounds of the mental health agencies. There seemed to be nothing for male abuse survivors. All the social services and support groups were for females. There was a men's group for abusers, but the closest male survivors' group was in Cornwall, nine hours away.

The only alternative was a private therapist, at about one hundred dollars an hour. Chris and I sat down and discussed finances for the first time, and came to some grim conclusions. Chris's Ontario Disability Support Program medical coverage didn't pay for therapy. I could help out until my unemployment insurance ended, and we could redirect some of Chris's rent money, but the kind of money we needed for any meaningful therapy could only come from one place: his family.

This was not good news. For Chris, one of the best things about living at my house was that his family couldn't get to him. His feelings about Eddie and Olga, in particular, swung between outrage and a cowed anxiety that they could still find a way to control his life.

Chris's family had not given up on him — far from it. Before Christmas, Eddie had phoned me several times, demanding to speak to him; I had repeatedly explained that Chris didn't feel that he could cope with that right now, but I would be happy to keep the family updated. I finally met with Eddie to explain the situation to him. It turned out to be a manipulation marathon: he started out as the authoritative parent, then the worried father (he even cried), then the concerned friend warning me not to be taken in by Chris. "You can't believe everything he says. He tends to exaggerate, you know — heh, heh."

I remembered that exact chuckle from my first meeting with Eddie. It finally clicked that he had this speech memorized — that undercutting Chris's credibility was second nature for him.

The next family member at bat was Chris's sister, Janice. She phoned from Ottawa, and Chris spoke to her for a few minutes and then meekly handed me the phone. "My sister wants to talk to you."

This was my first direct contact with Janice, and I was cautiously hopeful. Janice had been the main member of the family to keep track of Chris in Ottawa. She'd been able to get him moved to Mississauga in the first place, and the family seemed to respect her opinions. If we could get her on board, she could be a valuable ally in dealing with the others.

Janice had a brisk, take-charge voice, unusually mature for a twenty-year-old. She must have had to grow up fast in that family. "Hello, Mary, I've been meaning to talk to you. I've been busy at university, but Chris and I saw each other at my aunt's house over Christmas. He said that he's pretty happy staying with you. I appreciate everything you're doing for my brother."

"Well, Chris is a pretty remarkable person, and I'm happy to be able to help him. Actually, that's something I'd like to talk to you about—"

"I was wondering what plans you have for Chris, for a place to live. I know my aunt was trying to get him into a group home with your agency, something like where he was living before, with Barbara. That was a really good place you set up; I liked Barbara a lot."

I wondered if anyone had been keeping Janice informed; she didn't sound as if she knew about the suicide attempt or the hospitalizations. "I don't think Chris wants to move anywhere else at this point, Janice, and he's very welcome here. Actually, it may be kind of important for him to stay here; that's what I wanted to talk to you about. Chris has been pretty sick lately, and he's been getting a lot of memories coming back, about things you might not be aware of."

"You know, you can't always go by what Chris tells you. He tends to exaggerate, heh, heh."

I didn't just hear that. A sick chill went up my backbone.

"To tell you the truth, Janice, I haven't found that at all. I believe Chris."

Dead air on the phone line for a few seconds. I decided to push my momentary advantage. "He's been recovering memories about his teens, and some of them are about your stepmother, Ursula. I'm not sure how much you know about this, but Ursula was very abusive to Chris. He's been diagnosed with post-traumatic stress disorder, and he's going to need therapy—"

"That's ridiculous!" Janice was getting her second wind. "We only lived with Ursula for a year, maybe less. How could she have done anything to make him need therapy in that amount of time?"

I was taken aback — Chris had remembered staying with Ursula for at least three or four years. For a moment, I wasn't sure what to believe. Then I remembered something.

"Wait a minute, Janice, I saw the school psychiatrist's report on Chris; the agency needed it to document his disability. He was fourteen at the time, and Ursula's signature was on it. You had to have lived with her for at least two or three years by then."

More dead air.

"You were pretty young yourself, you probably don't remember exactly. But Ursula did a lot of damage, and we need help for Chris to get over it. Professional help, like a therapist. But therapy is expensive … Chris said that your grandfather might be in a position to help financially. Do you think that he could help?"

"I don't know." Janice sounded sullen; apparently the conversation wasn't going the way she had planned it.

"Well, your family seems to think a lot of you, and I was hoping that you could discuss the situation with your grandfather."

"Why doesn't Chris do it himself?"

"I think he feels very nervous discussing things with your grandfather."

"Well, I don't feel that it's my place to do it. If Chris wants something, he should ask for it himself." I could almost hear Janice sticking her tongue out at the other end of the phone line. The mature twenty-year-old had collapsed into a petulant brat. So much for the valuable ally.

We signed off with the standard pleasantries, and I hung up the phone feeling like I had been in a fistfight. If five minutes of dealing with Chris's family wore me out this badly, I wondered, what would a lifetime of it do to someone?

The only person left to ask for help was Chris's grandfather, a Hungarian refugee who came to Canada in 1963 and became a self-made millionaire. Chris had visited him frequently as a child, and a few times as a teenager; while it wasn't exactly a warm relationship, Eddie Sr. had often promised to be there for him if he ever needed anything. He could certainly afford to pay for Chris's therapy if he wanted to. And Janice did have a point: it was up to Chris to ask for help.

But Chris was too ashamed to face him. Eddie Sr. had been very critical of Chris's being unemployed when he got sick, and he had pushed hardest for Chris to just get back to work. He had not been sympathetic about the physical and emotional abuse, and Chris was not about to tell him about the sexual abuse. Convincing Eddie Sr. that therapy was even necessary was going to be an uphill battle, one that Chris wasn't ready to fight.

That left me to face Eddie Sr., if we were going to get anywhere. After my years as a social worker, not much intimidated me; still, I knew that Dan and Denise had shaken him down for support money when Chris was living with them, and that put me in a bad position to be asking for anything. There was no alternative, though; I sucked up all my nerve and made the call.

It was an easier conversation than I'd expected.

The voice on the line was firm and businesslike (helped along by a strong Hungarian accent), but not hostile. In fact, Eddie Sr. thought I'd been a great help to Chris and he agreed to meet with me the next day.

I hung up feeling pretty confident about the meeting. When I told Chris, he smiled but looked a bit sceptical. "I don't know, but I guess all he can say is 'no.' Just don't tell him too much about things, okay? I don't want Eddie and Olga knowing my business."

"Chris, stop worrying. You're here now. Your family has no control over your life anymore." (Yes, dear reader, by now you know that those were famous last words.)

One of my favourite movies is *The Lost Boys*, a vampire story with humour, action, romance, and a hot saxophone player — what more can you ask for? At the end, the brothers kill off all the vampires but one — the strongest, who created all the others. Little did I know that my appointment would be a replay of the movie climax: the meeting with the head vampire.

I wore a suit and high heels that I hadn't worn since quitting the agency: in this situation I suddenly felt the need to power-dress. The office was in a small industrial mall, not particularly impressive. Eddie Logan Sr. was in his shirt sleeves behind an old metal desk surrounded by filing cabinets and bookcases. He was smaller than I had expected, and certainly looked his eighty years. But as I entered he rose briskly from his desk and shook my hand firmly. He offered me a chair, and we sat for a moment, sizing each other up.

"So I understand that my grandson is living with you. Could I get your address and phone number?" He pulled out an empty file folder, labelled it "Christopher Logan," and slid a blank sheet on top of it. I gave my name and address like a job applicant, wondering if this was a power play. If so, he was damn good.

"I don't understand why my grandson did not come with you. He has not talked to his father or his aunt either, not for months. I don't understand what he is doing, but it is not right."

"This is kind of hard to understand, I know, but Chris is very sick right now." I had rehearsed this, but it wasn't coming out easily. This man probably had a flat-earth concept of mental illness. "I don't know if Olga or Eddie told you that Chris tried to kill himself last October, and he has been in the hospital several times since. He's seeing a psychiatrist, and she says that he has post-traumatic stress disorder… Some very bad things have happened to him, and he's starting to remember them and deal with them. It's taking some time, and it will also take some professional help."

"Christopher should talk to me about this himself. I don't understand why he did not come to see me for this."

"Chris is having a hard time talking to anyone right now. That's why I thought it was better if I came to explain things to you."

"I thank you for your concern, but my grandson should be with his family."

"That's his choice, and for now he feels more comfortable at my home. He's welcome there, and we're happy to have him. I know that he loves his family, but right now it's just very hard for him to face you. It's very stressful for him."

Eddie Sr. snorted. "Christopher has always been weak. His mother spoiled him; he did not get any discipline as a boy. He should grow up. He needs to go back to work and be a man."

"Chris can't go back to work until his psychiatrist says he can. I've already explained this to his aunt and his father." My social-worker persona was starting to crack. "He's on disability, but we aren't able to take care of his psychotherapy. This is what he needs if he is going to get well enough to work again."

"Why does he need all this? His sister is working and going to university. Even Christopher, when he lived with those people in Ottawa, he worked at a job. He is not smart, but he can work. This is all foolishness he is making."

"'Those people in Ottawa' treated him like a slave and took all his money. Didn't Olga tell you that they ran up debts under his name and that collection agencies were calling her house when he moved in?"

"That is what he told her. But Christopher is not smart, not good with money, so maybe this is not all true either."

I could see that this conversation was going nowhere fast, and the smart thing to do would have been to end it. But I was just too frigging mad by now.

"Christopher is not making up being sick. We have a report from a psychiatrist stating that he has PTSD. All I'm asking is for you to help your grandson by paying for his therapy—"

"I think maybe it is better if I find a therapist for Christopher myself."

That was a bluff — he would no sooner make an appointment with a psychologist than with a voodoo witch doctor. But it was a misstep — he had agreed in principle — and he quickly realized it.

"But what is there for Christopher to talk so much about? Maybe his life is not so easy, but his sister has had the same life and she is in university—"

"It wasn't the same thing. A lot of things happened to him that you don't know about. When Eddie was married to Ursula, he was drunk all the time so even he doesn't know how badly Ursula treated Chris." I was skating close to the edge, I knew, but I had it under control. "But she treated him very badly. That is the biggest reason he's sick right now. He's remembering a lot of things that happened back then, and he needs help to get over them."

I couldn't believe what happened next. Eddie Sr. got this indulgent smile across his face, and chuckled. "But Christopher exaggerates, heh, heh. You cannot believe everything he says."

Did they pass out a damn script or something? I lost it, and that's my only excuse for the words that came out of my mouth:

"Eddie, Ursula raped Chris."

He was shocked — for about five seconds. Then he looked down, cleared his throat, and said calmly, "Oh, no, I don't think so."

M. Scott Peck wrote in *People of the Lie* that normal people, faced with real evil, feel disoriented and confused. I actually felt the room tilt. I never wanted to get out of a place so badly; I thought I was going to throw up.

But it wasn't going to be that easy to leave. Eddie Sr. suddenly got to his feet with a vigor that was shocking in an eighty-year-old man, and began to pace back and forth in front of me as if he would have physically attacked me, had he dared. I could smell the anger coming off him.

"Christopher is my grandson, and you have no right to interfere with my family! I am going to Community Services and make a complaint. I will have you fired!"

"I don't work for them anymore," I pointed out.

"Then I will get to a lawyer and sue you! You have no right to keep my grandson. I make you give him back to his family! Who do you think you are dealing with?!?"

"You have no legal right to force Chris to do anything. Your lawyer will tell you that. I think we're through here."

"We are not through! You will see!" Those were the last words I heard as I walked out the door.

Chris later told me that when I got home, I looked like I'd been in a car crash. I had seen the real face of this family, the monster who beat his wife and terrorized his children, whose son had grown up to abuse his own family and drink himself nearly to death, whose daughter and granddaughter had learned the role of accomplice from their cradles. Chris alone had escaped the family curse and had fallen instead into the role of scapegoat. No wonder they wanted him back so badly; he was the counterweight in the family balance, the target for their hatred that would otherwise fall back on themselves and eat them alive.

We finally decided to get a therapist and see how long we could afford to pay for treatment ourselves; if the money ran out, it ran out. In the meantime, Chris was developing another symptom: hallucinations.

Chapter Twenty-Two

It Was Funnier When Cary Grant Did It

There is a Cary Grant movie, *Topper*, about a butler who is haunted by the ghosts of his late employers. It's a comedy, of course: the ghosts keep distracting him as he tries to go through his normal life, and people around him think he's talking to himself, and so on. The situation isn't so funny in real life — especially when the people haunting you are your abusers.

At first, Chris was seeing fuzzy figures in the mirror when he shaved or brushed his teeth. (These were the only times he was willing to look in a mirror; he had a phobia about reflections.) He described them as outlines of human beings, but filled in with static, like television screens when the cable is down. Then the static outlines became "real" and began to follow Chris around. Finally, they coalesced into solid, three-dimensional versions of Ursula and Jacques.

Chris would see them naked, Jacques with a hard-on, jerking off, laughing at him. They were so real that he could see freckles on Ursula and the lines on the palms of Jacques's hands — "He had a lot of lines on his hands just like I do." They told him he was stupid, that getting raped was all he was good for. Sometimes they told him to kill himself.

"It's hard to hear other people talking over them," he said. "And they're solid, like real people. If you walk behind where they are, I can't see you. I know they aren't real, but it doesn't make any difference."

He said they showed up everywhere and closed in on him, getting right in his face. When they surrounded him so he couldn't see anything else, he would go into a full flashback. That's why he got so distracted when we went out — he was trying to ignore them as much as he could.

It was getting very difficult for Chris to go out of the house at all, even with me. He soon gave up staying downstairs in the apartment he was so proud of and started sleeping on the living room couch. Apparently, the one place the hallucinations couldn't show up was on the main floor of our house. Chris would sit in the living room and describe them standing in the doorway to the basement, angry about being kept out.

After a month or so, Chris couldn't stay alone in the house at all. If he was by himself for more than an hour, the hallucinations would start to sneak upstairs and overwhelm him. He could spend hours in flashback until someone came home. He was trapped in a weird nexus between the present and the nightmare past that kept sucking him back in. His life went from a day-to-day struggle for sanity to a minute-by-minute fight for the most basic connection to reality. The only time he felt safe was when I was with him. We found that if we could joke about the hallucinations or make fun of them, they would disappear for a while. Chris would tell me when he saw them, and we would laugh at Ursula's chicken legs or Jacques's pregnancy gut. Humour was the only thing that could ground Chris in the here-and-now. And if it failed, I could stop him from going into a flashback by hugging and reassuring him.

We were more and more desperate for a therapist, but no one wanted to take on someone as sick as Chris, or someone with PTSD, or a male abuse survivor. It was ironic that the sicker you were, the less help was available to you.

Finally, I found a therapist who had treated PTSD and was willing to take Chris. We went to the first interview at her new office, a nice professional nook with a New Age vibe. It suited Dr. Amiel's personality well.

I did most of the talking during the intake, while Chris quietly dissociated on the sofa. Dr. Amiel seemed to take things in stride, until I explained how to deal with his flashbacks. She wasn't comfortable with bear-hugging a client, so we arranged that I would stay in the office during Chris's sessions, for such emergencies.

"So, Chris," Dr. Amiel turned to the sofa, where Chris had appeared to be sleeping. He calmly opened his eyes, as if he had been involved the whole time. "What would you like to accomplish during therapy?"

"I don't know, to get well, I guess." The question seemed to depress him. "I don't know if that's ever going to happen, though. My life is so messed up, I don't think there's anything I can do about it." His head slumped down between his shoulders, and he seemed to deflate. I saw a flashback on the way, and figured it was as good a time as any to break in the new therapist, so I intervened.

"Chris, look at me, honey." I knelt in front of him and took his hands, making eye contact as I talked him down. "I know it feels hopeless, but right now is the worst part; it's going to get better, I promise... Do you remember your Uncle Pierre, and the accident he was in? He lost an eye, and the doctors had to rebuild his face. Can you imagine how he felt when he woke up after the accident, like he would never get better?"

"Yeah, I guess."

"How does he look now?"

"He looks fine. They fixed everything, you can't even tell anything ever happened."

"That's going to be you someday. This new therapist, and Dr. Vindar, and us talking at home, it's all part of getting better. It's hard, I know, but you can do it, you're my little superhero."

Chris took a deep breath, and I saw the wheels turning in his brain as he digested this idea. More importantly, the flashback had been averted by changing his focus to something else. I got up off the floor and back in my armchair. Dr. Amiel had been watching the event with some interest; this was probably not the usual intake interview process. But she picked up where she left off, discussing fees and session schedules. Chris was scheduled for a battery of psychological assessments, and we said goodbye and left.

One benefit of having a therapist was that Chris could now be referred to the Trauma Assessment Program at Mount Sinai Hospital in Toronto; they didn't take referrals unless a therapist is involved. At Chris's next appointment, Dr. Vindar started the process, which meant putting Chris on their waiting list.

We also introduced Dr. Amiel to Chris's imaginary entourage, Ursula and Jacques, who were attending the session as well. Apparently, this was a new phenomenon to her: she questioned Chris closely about how they looked and sounded to him, and what he thought about them. I knew she was considering the possibility of schizophrenia, which also involves hallucinations. However, schizophrenia is a thought process disorder, involving delusions as well; the person believes in their hallucinations. Chris was quite clear that he was "seeing things," which made him too sane for the diagnosis. Dr. Amiel explained that Chris was actually having a type of flashback rather than a true hallucination. Still, she prescribed an antipsychotic to try counteracting the symptoms. It calmed Chris down, but had no effect on the constant presence of Ursula and Jacques.

CHAPTER TWENTY-THREE

WE'RE FROM THE AGENCY

For thirteen years, I had a love-hate relationship with my job at Community Services: I loved the work and the client families, and hated the agency I worked for. John McKnight once wrote that "social service agencies exist to give employment to social workers," and that is a perfect description of the agency when I was there. It hadn't always been that way; in the beginning, families of institutionalized children with disabilities started a non-profit organization in order to bring their children home and to get help from the government to take care of them at home and in the community. I wish I had been working for the agency then; that would have been inspiring. But as time went on, professionals were hired to run the organization, and Ministry funding became Ministry control, and the agency became less and less concerned with serving its client families, and more and more concerned with protecting its resources from them. Staff who didn't go along with the agenda were forced out one way or another. Finally, Community Services entered its current incarnation as an ossified relic of its original intent.

When I joined the agency, I was naive enough to believe everything I was told in orientation, and I fell in love with my job. Previously, I had worked as a psychometrist for a school board, and it had been interesting to analyze learning disabilities and recommend changes in teaching strategies — and frustrating to see my reports stuck in files that never again saw the light of day.

This job was perfect for me. I met a family, analyzed their situation, developed a plan with them to access resources, then went out and got the resources, made sure the problems were solved, and monitored the situation to make sure things worked out. On one level, it was like working out puzzles; on a deeper level, I came to admire the people who sacrificed so much for their children in such frustrating and thankless circumstances. My client families were my heroes, and there was no excitement like watching a family get the help they needed after years, sometimes, of living with terrible hardships.

Needless to say, my attitude was not shared by all my coworkers, who were nice people but not out to make waves. They looked at my efforts, and worried that somebody was going to ask them to work that hard; after all, "families talk, you know, Mary." The fact that I was enjoying myself so damn much probably rubbed salt in the wounds; I had to ride out a period of severe unpopularity, and was finally written off as the agency eccentric and left alone to do as I pleased. I was also the dumping ground for the really difficult cases, which was fine by me. I enjoyed reviewing my case files like a master gardener enjoys a stroll through the greenhouse.

Of course, the downside was the amount of work involved. I put in twelve hour days on a regular basis, did home visits on weekends and holidays, and even dreamed about work. It may have been a miracle that I made it through thirteen years, but for a year or so before Chris came, I was starting to feel like a boxer who was getting knocked down more, and having a harder and harder time getting up off the mat. My memory was shot; I had to write everything down. I was always tired; on the weekends I could sleep as much as twenty-four hours at a time. I lived on caffeine, donuts, and antidepressants.

But it wasn't the work with the families that was draining me so badly: it was the agency's attitude. Originally, they provided group homes and sheltered workshops for intellectually disabled clients. When there were more clients than places, and no funding to create more places, they created case management, summer activities, and respite programs for people who still had their family members at home, but the Ministry didn't provide much funding for this area, and the agency treated it as something of an afterthought, even when we began serving hundreds of families. Resources that could have been stretched to cover our client families were hoarded to support the "hard services." Our families became the enemy, the insurgents who were invading the well-run citadel of Community Services.

To save money, case managers were told to reduce home visits and answer questions over the phone when possible. On the other hand, we were to formally document each contact with families; a one-minute phone call often precipitated five minutes of progress notes. I knew that this was going to result in useless service at best, and disasters at worst, and I refused to change my style of case-management. The writing was on the wall from then on. I knew my days were numbered, but I went down fighting.

Even after I quit, the agency and I kept butting heads over my continued involvement with Chris. When they had meetings, they told Chris that I couldn't attend even if he invited me. I told them to put it in writing, and they shut up — they knew that Chris could have anyone he wanted at his meetings, and they knew that I knew. Still, I was as welcome as a hooker at a prayer meeting. Since there was nothing they could offer him, the contacts dwindled, and I assumed that his case had gone inactive.

Which is why I was a bit suspicious when, out of the blue, we got a phone call from Chris's caseworker, Kelly, informing us that his application for residential funding had been approved. Of course, Chris no longer needed a residential placement; but if we could access some of the funding, his therapy would be covered. When Kelly asked for a case conference, we agreed. I was cautiously optimistic and frankly curious.

The assortment of old acquaintances that showed up for the case conference gave me mixed feelings from the start. On the plus side, there was one of my old supervisors, Ryan, a sincerely good-hearted man who had gone into social services from the seminary thirty years previously. He had helped with the original residential funding application, and Chris knew and trusted him. On the minus side was Martha, another residential supervisor, scrawny, bitter, and poisonous as a mandrake root. In-between was Chris's case manager and my old co-worker, Kelly, a by-the-book-and-cover-your-ass type who inspired in me neither confidence nor concern.

We met downstairs around Chris's dining room table. I made sure that Chris told them I could speak for him; I wasn't sure he could hold his own at this meeting, and I had seen other clients "participated" into decisions they didn't understand or agree to.

Ryan started the meeting by telling us that the agency had received funding to help set Chris up in his own place. "We're here to talk about what that should look like. I know you were pretty independent at Barbara's place—"

I stopped him right there. "Ryan, I don't know if you've been kept up to date on the situation; but first of all, Chris's needs have changed drastically over the last six months, and second, he wants to live here. I've been taking care of him for four months, and this is his home now. He doesn't want to move."

Martha piped up, "I think we need to hear that from Chris," and three pairs of eyes lasered in on Chris, who shrivelled in his chair. I knew that he was about to dissociate, which was the last thing we needed, so I put my arm around him and made eye contact.

"Chris, just tell them what you want. It's okay. No one can make you leave if you don't want to."

"I need to use the washroom." And the meeting was held up for about five minutes with the painful sound of Chris retching his guts out.

Since I knew that Chris could be quite a while in there, I took the opportunity to explain the changes in his situation. "Even if he wanted to leave, which he doesn't, the plan we made six months ago isn't appropriate anymore. He's had a suicide attempt, he's been hospitalized twice, he hallucinates, he has fainting spells — he can't be left alone!"

Martha retorted, "I don't think there's anything that needs to be changed in the original plan. He was doing fine at Barbara's—"

"Suicide attempt!" I nearly yelled it in her face.

"I don't think you need to use that tone of voice in this meeting. We are all here to do the best for Chris, and I think you could be a bit more cooperative," Kelly said, and I was startled into silence at being scolded in my own house.

Chris came back from the washroom looking a little green but fairly focused. I decided to put forward a plan of my own. "Why don't I apply to be a foster parent through the agency for Chris? You can supervise the residential placement, and Chris can keep living here." And we would have our therapy money.

Immediate silence. Ryan was ready with an answer — too ready. "We don't think that would be a good idea," he recited, "since you worked for the agency so recently and you were his caseworker. We feel that it wouldn't be ethical."

"Okay, then would you at least allow him to live here, and provide some funding or supports for him? I could use some relief, and we need funding for his therapy—"

"No, we would not be willing to be involved in any arrangement involving him living here."

Chris bolted from the table and ran into the kitchen. The group around the dining room table looked shocked; I got up and followed him. Chris was crying uncontrollably behind the kitchen door.

I put my arms around him. "Chris, this is your home and they have nothing to say about it. You're not going anywhere. They can keep their damn money, we never asked for it and we don't need it. Don't worry about it. This is your home!"

By the time he had calmed down, the group around the table had begun to pack up. "We think that it might be better to do this another time, when Chris is feeling better," Ryan said. I agreed, and Chris started crying again from relief. Ryan, the last to leave, stopped at the top of the stairs. "Are you going to be all right?"

"We've managed for four months," I replied tartly.

Ryan had the decency to look embarrassed. "Chris, if you need to talk, you can call me, okay?"

Chris nodded politely, and Ryan left. The aftertaste of the meeting lingered, however, and I knew enough about case conferences to recognize something very wrong about this one. These people had come with a definite agenda: to get Chris out of my house and into a group home.

What went on afterwards was even stranger. Kelly started meeting with Chris to discuss his situation, but wouldn't meet at our house. They had to meet at the nearby Tim Hortons. I came along when Chris wanted me, which was most of the time, and I tried to explain about Chris's PTSD symptoms and why his support needs were different. I honestly didn't expect any change in the decision; I assumed that Kelly was maintaining contact with Chris to make things look good.

That was until one meeting when I dropped Chris off at Timmy's and saw Martha sitting at the table with Kelly. I parked and got in there fast. The meeting was mostly about Chris's dog, and it ended fairly quickly. The next time, Kelly and Martha brought a new collar for Hazzard. Martha went out for a smoke break with Chris during the meeting, and he seemed uncomfortable when they came back. Later, he told me that Martha had been trying to discourage him from bringing me to the meetings: "You aren't joined to Mary at the hip, are you, heh, heh." Chris was extremely sensitive to manipulation, especially the "heh, heh" type, and this worried him.

I knew things were getting really bizarre, however, when Martha and Kelly showed up at my door one morning without calling to set up a meeting. I had been up all night with Chris, who was finally asleep, and I had just dropped off myself when the doorbell rang.

"Is Chris in? We thought we'd take him out to lunch."

I was still groggy. "Chris didn't tell me about a lunch date. He just fell asleep. When did you set this up?"

"We were just in the area and we thought we'd come by and see him."

"You have the number here, you could have called first."

Martha and Kelly looked at each other. Then Kelly said, "Well, there's no phone downstairs, and we weren't sure you would give him the message. We aren't really comfortable having to go through you to contact Chris."

I had hit my limit. "Look, there is one phone in this house, and Chris gets any message you leave for him. And I don't know what's going on, but don't you show up at my door again without calling!" I slammed the door in their faces and went back to bed. Now, of course, I was too mad to sleep. Something weird was going on — nobody showed up at a client's house without an appointment, ever. For some reason, they were determined to get at Chris. And after four months of not giving a damn, it made no sense that they were so hell-bent on it now.

It was time to take the bull by the horns: I phoned the agency and asked for a meeting with Martha's supervisor. To my surprise, I ended up with the Residential Director and the Executive Director sitting on my living room sofa.

CHAPTER TWENTY-FOUR
PAY NO ATTENTION TO THE
MAN BEHIND THE CURTAIN

Brenda, the Residential Director, was tall, thin, and bleached blonde. She had probably been very attractive in her youth, and hadn't let go of the style: her hair was always in an up-do and sprayed into immobility, and her face had a lacquered smoothness. She looked like a life-sized Menopause Barbie. Her personality was as brittle and fake as her hair; I trusted her less than anyone else at the agency.

Sherman, the Executive Director, was short and nondescript except for a Burton Cummings–style moustache that tried a bit too hard to compensate. He was an ex-accountant who lived in fear that someone was going to hold him accountable for something. His presence here meant that there was some kind of political pressure being put on the agency to complete Chris's placement. It seemed odd that the Ministry would be this involved.

We had the meeting upstairs in the living room. Brenda had enthroned herself on the sofa while Sherman burrowed into the armchair. Chris huddled next to me on the loveseat, as far from them as he could get.

I began the meeting by describing the impromptu visit the previous week, but Brenda interrupted: "We came here to discuss Chris's living situation. The Ministry has provided the funding for a placement, and we're trying to set up a living arrangement for Chris. I don't see why you're making it difficult for us to do our jobs."

"Chris has a home here, and he's repeatedly told your staff that he wants to stay here. If you don't want to fund this situation, fine. But you and I both know that you have no power to remove Chris if he doesn't want to go, and I'm willing for him to stay. And I want your staff to stop trying to coerce him. What they're doing is unethical and you know it."

Sherman spoke up from the far side of the room: "I'm concerned about the position you've put the agency in with your handling of this case. You had no authority to set up a residential placement at Barbara's house. That's got us involved with everything that happened there, and the family's very upset about it."

So there it was! Chris's family was using the agency to get him back! I had told Eddie Sr. that he had no legal basis for compelling Chris to do anything, and that was true. But Community Services had worked with families so often to plan for their clients, they lost sight sometimes of the fact that those families had no legal status unless the person was declared incompetent in a court hearing. Most families don't do this, and the clients don't care if their families plan for them. But in Chris's case, they knew that they were working against his wishes. This was totally unethical. But it still made sense; all Eddie Sr. had to do was threaten to sue the agency. With Sherman, it was like a Pavlovian response: say the word "lawsuit" and the man lost bladder control.

"Sherman, the agency was not involved in the arrangements with Barbara. That was between Chris and Barbara. He rented a basement apartment from her independently. I drafted the agreement; there was nothing about Community Services in it. I stayed involved as his caseworker, that's all. And right now, may I remind you, I don't work for you. Whatever arrangement I make with Chris for living here has nothing to do with the agency, either. If you want to set up a foster-care arrangement with me, I'll consider it. If you want to send in-home care for Chris, I could use the break. Otherwise, keep your money, and I'll keep Chris."

Sherman backed down into his chair, and Brenda roared into the battle: "How ethical was it for you to take over like this, considering how vulnerable Chris is? You were his case manager; it wasn't your business to move him into your home like this. How do we know that this is what Chris wants?"

"Because he told you?"

"We haven't heard anything from Chris, actually." She looked past me to Chris, who was hunched into himself with his eyes on the ground. He wasn't dissociating, though; he was sticking with it. I was proud of him.

"Chris," Sherman leaned forward in his chair, "we'd like to hear what you want."

Chris struggled silently with the words for several minutes.

"When I lived at Barbara's, I tried to tell her how I felt about things. She wouldn't listen to me. She just listened to my dad and my Aunt Olga, and did whatever they said. I didn't feel like it mattered what I wanted."

I was used to Chris's roundabout way of expressing himself; he was afraid to confront situations in the present, so he'd find a similar situation in his past and bring it up. "Chris, are you worried that people won't listen to you, like Barbara, because of your family?"

Chris looked at me and nodded.

"Well, the first thing you have to do is say what you want, or you never find out if people will listen or not. These people need to hear from you where you want to live. Can you tell them?"

Chris looked firmly across at Sherman, and said, "I like living here. Mary is like my second mother. I don't want to move."

Sherman sat back, not necessarily satisfied but thoroughly checkmated, and contemplated the coming legal action. Brenda wasn't done, however.

"But how are you so sure that you're qualified? If Chris is so sick, he should be taken care of by professionals. You don't know what you're doing. Kelly's been staying in contact with Chris, and she has concerns about your treatment of Chris."

"She has *what*?"

"She is concerned about how you discuss Chris's experiences with her. She feels that you seem to enjoy talking about it."

My jaw dropped to my kneecaps. I had no idea how Kelly could have come up with an idea like that. I'd used humour to relax Chris during the meetings at Tim Hortons, but the possibility that I was *enjoying* hearing about these horrors day after day? "I think we're done here. You don't have anything to offer, and this situation is just getting too offensive. Please don't contact us again."

Even after they left, the idea of Kelly believing that I enjoyed talking about Chris's abuse still made me uncomfortable. I don't have an emotionally demonstrative personality, and this actually helped me with my work; people could tell me heartbreaking stories of their lives, and I could stay focused on resolving the problems rather than being affected by them. Even Chris never felt that what he was telling me was too much for me. We could joke about the memories, and that seemed to help Chris get control over them.

But, at some level, Chris's stories did hold a peculiar fascination for me. I had read in one of the PTSD manuals that helpers had to be careful not to push victims for details, and I remembered doing this with Chris from time to time out of a ghoulish curiosity. I think we all have that tendency, buried in our crocodile brains — that carrion appetite for cruelty or horror. Movie companies make fortunes on this appetite with monsters and serial killers; people like Ursula and Jacques satisfy their urges more directly. If I wasn't going to damage Chris as well, it was important for me to recognize this tendency and guard against it.

I was also starting to understand Chris's pessimistic view of the world. Even with my low opinion of Community Services, I had expected them to behave ethically at the very least. I was beginning to understand that the world behaves very differently to people who don't have the power to hold it accountable. And it was a cold and uncomfortable realization.

CHAPTER TWENTY-FIVE

YOU ARE GETTING SLEEPY...

We kept up with the therapist on our own resources, and she helped by charging us the minimum fee. Chris had weekly sessions, and I stayed nearby in case he needed help. Dr. Amiel began by giving Chris a battery of psychological tests, which confirmed the diagnosis of profound PTSD. The therapy, however, looked a lot like Chris's talks with me every night on the sofa. I began to realize that, at an hour per week and seventy dollars per hour, Chris would be fifty years old by the time he was done, and therapy would have cost over one hundred thousand dollars. There was just too much material to cover. But we had no other options.

Actually, we did try one other therapy: hypnosis. I saw an ad for a hypnotherapist in the newspaper and wondered if it might help some of Chris's symptoms. Getting rid of the constant hallucinations would be worth any price; and even if Chris could just stop vomiting all the time, it would be a big step forward.

The hypnotherapist's office was in the basement of his house; a side door led to a small room, boarded off with plywood and old curtains to create a private area. Chris sat in a recliner, and Larry the hypnotherapist and I sat on mismatched kitchen chairs. Larry was as casual as his surroundings, in sweatshirt and jeans and an old pair of sneakers. Chris felt more comfortable with him than with Dr. Amiel, so I figured we had nothing to lose by trying — except a hundred dollars a session.

The first session began with relaxation exercises, which seemed to make Chris very tense. Larry was able to talk Chris down, and spent an hour trying to implant suggestions. Chris kept tensing up; I could tell, even if he was trying to look "out of it" to appease Larry.

Later, I asked him what was going on. Chris admitted that he had been too nervous to focus on the hypnotic suggestions. "Jacques had these tapes, and he used to listen to them and do relaxation exercises in his basement. I would stand there until he was done, and then he would rape me."

"So the relaxation exercises are triggering rape memories. This could be a problem."

Chris let me do the explaining; Larry was very sympathetic, but agreed that hypnosis wouldn't work very well under the circumstances. But he wasn't willing to give up yet: "I have a friend who has experience with trauma patients. Maybe she can give me some ideas."

The next week, Larry was ready for us with pages of notes from his friend.

Chris settled in the recliner, Larry darkened the room, and I sat back quietly on my kitchen chair. Then Larry began to read from his notes.

"We call upon Saint Michael the Archangel, who banished Satan from the heavenly realm, to eject all evil and malign spirits in this room. Rescue this man from the evil forces which torment him. And we thank Saint Michael for his help…"

I nearly fell off my chair trying to stifle my laughter. Larry was trying to exorcise the trauma memories!

Actually, as I thought about it, the idea made some sense: like post-hypnotic suggestions, the exorcism ceremony might convince the subconscious to get rid of the traumatic hallucinations. I watched Chris; he still seemed stiff and uncomfortable, not really absorbing the process. I'm not sure why I did what I did next, but it seemed to come from my need to exorcise my own fury as much as Chris's fear.

I asked Larry if I could try talking to Ursula.

I stood beside Chris, and asked him where Ursula was standing. He pointed to a corner off to his right. I faced the corner, and let it rip: "Ursula, you perverted bitch, I've been listening for months to the things you've done to Chris. You're a mother, and you raped and tortured another woman's child. What were you thinking? Well, you have no power here. Chris is my son now, he is mine and you have nothing more to do with him. You can fuck off and go to hell."

I turned to Chris, who still had his eyes closed, and put my hand on his chest. "Chris, I love you and I'm proud of you, and no one is ever going to hurt you again. You're my son now. I know you to the bottom of your soul, and you are a good, good person and you are going to have the life you deserve. I promise you."

I stopped, exhausted; Chris was watching me in amazement, and when I looked over at Larry, I was surprised to see tears in his eyes. I suddenly felt very self-conscious, and suggested that we stop the session early. Larry turned the lights on, and I remembered that I'd left my purse in the car. I took a few extra minutes to collect myself, then went back in to pay Larry.

On the way home, Chris told me that Larry had talked to him while I had been outside: he'd said that he was absolutely sure that Chris was going to get well. He also gave him a bit of advice that was probably worth more than any therapy at the time: He told Chris to do things that made him happy.

We never went back to Larry, since the hypnotherapy had no effect on Chris's symptoms, but that last bit of advice was pure genius. We started finding small things that Chris wanted, and we got them for him. He developed a collection of movie DVDs and a music collection of heavy metal CDs, and I would find them in the morning spread out in the living room; when Chris couldn't sleep, he sat up and gloated over his new possessions like a miser over his gold. He told me, "It's so fucking great. I want something, and I can get it, and it's mine! Nobody can take it or yell at me for having it. It's amazing!" These little pieces of plastic gave Chris the first taste of real control over his life, and all of them together probably cost less than three hours of therapy.

The traditional therapy, on the other hand, was going at a snail's pace. Chris had me stay in the room for some of the sessions, and they were covering topics that Chris and I had talked to death six months earlier. Dr. Amiel was in no hurry to get to the sexual abuse issues, and Chris was in no hurry to bring them up with her. The heavy therapy was still going on at two o'clock in the morning on our living room sofa. But that didn't count; we needed Dr. Amiel in order to qualify for the other available resources.

Finally, Chris's referral to the Trauma Assessment Program came through. I had been hoping it was a treatment program; as it turned out, they merely assessed the patient and made treatment suggestions to the therapist. That was why the patient needed to be involved with a therapist; patients who couldn't afford one didn't need assessing, apparently, since they had no way to benefit from the program's sage advice. Still, it was all we had, so Chris made his intake appointment.

Since Chris had a hard time explaining things, I wrote a five-page summary of his history and current symptoms to give to his assessor. She was impressed by the professional quality of the report, and it did speed up the process quite a bit. I stayed with Chris through the battery of tests, mostly question-and-answer in format. One section of the test fascinated me: it involved questions about extrasensory perception, and particularly experiences of "possession." Nothing I had read had ever mentioned a connection between PTSD and ESP/paranormal experiences. A month later, I had reason to remember this issue.

The second part of the assessment was an interview with the psychiatrist, Dr. Ulrich. He was supposed to be an authority on PTSD; I thought he was a bit spacey, but it was part of the assessment. Dr. Ulrich noticed that Chris would participate when I was out of the room, but became silent when I was there. I was surprised at this, and Dr. Ulrich warned me not to let Chris become too dependent on me. Chris heard this, and later had a total meltdown thinking I was going to abandon him. He explained that he could put up a front with people, it was how he survived all those years, but that he let down his front when I was there because he was safe with me. Sometimes dependence is the first step toward getting well, because it involves being able to trust someone else. I reassured Chris that I believed him, and Dr. Ulrich went down several points in my estimation for his potentially destructive remark.

When our copy of the report came, Dr. Ulrich and the whole program went down a few hundred points. It was the most inaccurate and poorly-written piece of garbage I had ever seen. My own summary was used extensively, and misquoted frequently. The test results were reported, and supported a diagnosis of severe post-traumatic stress disorder (a level down from profound; I couldn't imagine what profound PTSD must look like if Chris was only "severe"). Even Dr. Amiel said, diplomatically, that she had been surprised by the recommendations. We chalked it up to experience, but the let-down depressed me for weeks.

The therapy sessions with Dr. Amiel limped on for another month or so, until the money finally ran out. Chris didn't seem terribly affected by the change, but letting go of our only therapy resource was unexpectedly upsetting for me.

I was beginning to understand that there was nothing out there that was going to help Chris get well. I was going to do it myself or it wasn't going to get done. Even when I had moved Chris in and realized how sick he was, I had always assumed that there was something out there available to him. As a caseworker, I had always been able to find resources for my clients: sometimes it took some heavy-duty scrounging and finessing, but I had always managed it. This time, there was flat-out nothing. The two of us were completely on our own. Chris was depending on me, and I had no idea of what to do. The situation I had seen a hundred times in client households had come home to roost on my own front porch, and I was helpless against it.

Chapter Twenty-Six

Can I Still Swim in It?

Until now, I'd had no trouble believing everything Chris told me; as grim as it got, the perpetrators were human. The next group of memories were the first ones to shake my faith in Chris's sanity. He began to remember seeing ghosts.

It started with a peculiar dream, even for Chris: "I was asleep in my bedroom at Ursula's house. I woke up, and there was someone in the bed with me. I could see a head on the pillow next to mine. It looked like a child's head, facing away from me so I could only see the back. I heard a kind of snore, then the person in the bed rolled over. It looked like a boy. But then it woke up, and it had black eyes and sharp, pointed teeth. That's when I woke up."

Besides the new dream, Chris was starting to be even more anxious and irritable than usual. This had become the warning sign for new memories. It was like the feeling of sickness before an attack of nausea: the actual vomiting is often a relief by comparison. When a new set of memories was about to shake loose, Chris would need to talk for hours, and he didn't get any calmer after talking. Everything upset him, and even Ativan wouldn't calm him down. It was nerve-wracking: he never knew what was coming, but he could be fairly sure it would be awful.

Finally, about two or three days after the dream, Chris stopped short in the middle of our nightly talk. He sat there for a few minutes with a look of almost hypnotic concentration. When he came to, he seemed unusually disturbed.

"Mom," he said, not meeting my gaze, "you know I'm not a liar, an exaggerator, or a bullshitter, right?" This was his mantra for ensuring he would be believed no matter what. I agreed, not really surprised — he asked this compulsively about forty times a day. But this time, he didn't look too reassured.

"Mom, this is going to sound crazy, but I'm not making it up. I think that house was haunted. I remember seeing ghosts there."

Of all the things Chris told me before or since, this was the only time I really faltered in believing him. One part of my brain was going, "*Omigod*, he really is crazy, what am I going to do now?" Chris must have read my mind, because he was ready for me.

"Mom, I wasn't the only one who saw them. Ursula had a priest over to bless the house three times. Janice saw a lady in a white dress once, she told me. Even Julio saw something: we found him out in the yard in his underwear in the middle of the night, muttering, 'They're coming, they're coming,' and it didn't sound like his voice at all. When we woke him up, he didn't remember anything but he didn't want to come back in the house. That was a weird house."

The fact that Chris was discussing the idea rationally reassured me. "Okay, honey, I believe you. So, what do you remember?"

"Well, the first ghost I saw was the Headless Lady. It was in the evening, and I was up in my bedroom looking out the window. I was having a smoke, and I always did it by the window so no one could smell it. Ursula would have given me shit if she caught me. I had a tin pie plate out on the window ledge for the butts.

"Anyway, my bedroom window faced the front of the house, and I could see the street and the sidewalk. I noticed this lady walking up the sidewalk toward our driveway. She was dressed funny, wearing an old-fashioned dress, a long one with lace on the front, but I didn't notice anything unusual about her other than that. Then she stopped at our driveway, like she was going to come up to the house. She looked up at my window, like she was looking right at me. Then I noticed, 'Holy shit, she doesn't have a head.' When she saw me looking at her, like she seemed to know I was there, she came right up off the ground and flew like she was going to come through the bedroom window at me. I ran out of my bedroom so fast I don't think I even touched the floor, it was like one big jump to the door. Then I ran downstairs, and I don't think I touched the stairs either, just right to the landing and then I hit the wall and just sat there."

"Was that the only time you saw a ghost at the house?"

Chris concentrated again, running his internal camcorder. "No, I saw her some other times, but usually inside the house. I would see her on the stairs sometimes, but she wasn't as solid, you could see through her. Sometimes she had a scarf or a veil or something around her head, and other times she didn't have a head. I could see a black hole between her shoulders, no bones or blood, but it was still creepy."

"Maybe you were hallucinating? This sounds a lot like Ursula and Jacques following you around, and you know they aren't real."

"No, it felt totally different. I got this cold scary feeling from being around her, and it doesn't feel like that with the hallucinations. I mean, you can tell when it's somebody else in the room with you."

I noticed that Chris was relating these memories exactly the way he told the others he had recovered: with a clinical attitude and a photographic attention to detail. Whatever they were about, they were real memories. I had to conclude that Chris had seen a ghost.

My own attitude toward the supernatural is neither belief nor disbelief, but a hardheaded look at the available evidence. Based on what I've read, there is no reason to dismiss the existence of ghosts: too many credible people have given eyewitness testimonies that could not be refuted. Chris was also a pretty hardheaded realist; he had to be in order to have survived. If he reported seeing a ghost, the only reason he would have is that he saw one. And it would have been safer for him not to tell me and risk my disbelief. For him to make up a story like this was unthinkable, and for him to have imagined it went against everything I knew about Chris.

Chris actually may have had a better chance than most people of developing psychic sensitivity, because of his abuse history. From what I've read, people who have had near-death experiences or severe traumas often reported increased psychic awareness. And ceremonies to produce mystic experiences tend to include discomfort, pain, or even life-threatening ordeals. They may also include drugs, and Chris was using marijuana regularly by then to cope with his abuse.

Chris spent three or four weeks unpacking this set of memories, and there were a lot of them: the house must have been an Amityville franchise. "I would go downstairs at night and smell cigarette smoke, but nobody smoked inside the house. Once or twice, I saw the tip of the cigarette burning in the dark, and when I turned on the light there was nothing there. Once, I saw the leather cushions on the sofa move, like somebody was sitting there and got up. Doors were always opening and closing with nobody around. That's around the time I started to get scared of mirrors: I kept seeing reflections of things that weren't in the room. Even shaving and brushing my teeth got nerve-wracking.

"I remember one time, I was making a peanut butter sandwich, and a rocking chair in the room started rocking with nobody in it. I was all by myself, and it was kind of scary, the chair just rocked harder and harder and then flipped over backwards. I stood the chair back up so Ursula wouldn't blame it on me, then I took my sandwich and got the hell out of there."

The dream about the terrifying child in bed with him kept repeating, night after night; this often meant a "stuck" memory, and we went over the dream again and again in our nightly talks. Finally, the memory popped out, and it was the most remarkable one that I had heard yet: the story of Chris's friend Henry.

"I was thirteen, it was a little while after Ursula had started in on me. I woke up one night because I was cold, and the covers were on the floor. I looked over the side of the bed, and there was this thing asleep on the floor, it looked like a deformed little child with a big bald head, and it had hogged the blankets. When I looked again, it had disappeared.

"I was getting really mad at the hauntings by now, and the next afternoon I went down to the laundry room where no one else could hear me. Then I yelled at the ghost, 'All right, here I am! You got beef with me, show yourself right now. I dare you, you pussy, fucking show yourself!'

"This figure appeared in front of me, with black eyes and sharp, pointy teeth, just like in the dream. I screamed 'You win!' and ran upstairs without looking behind me.

"A few days later, I was swimming in the backyard pool with my friend Chad from Trinidad. I looked over at the house, and I saw this boy standing there pointing down at the deep end of the pool. Then he disappeared. Chad didn't see him that time. After that, I would see him outside when I was swimming, and he would point at the pool. Sometimes his face was normal but with white eyes, no pupils, and other times it would look like it did in the dream.

"Finally, he showed up and Chad saw him too. He screamed, and then I screamed, and we both jumped over the hedge at the back of the yard. Chad ran for home, but I peeked back over the bushes. He was still there, and he was looking at me. He pointed to a little jewellery box that Janice had left out in the yard, then at himself, then at the pool. Then he disappeared.

"A couple of days later, I came home from school, and when I closed the front door, he was behind me in the foyer. His face had the black eyes and pointy teeth like in the dream. He just stood there.

"I stood there too, for a minute, totally freaked. But I figured that the best way to handle this was to stay calm, so I said, 'Hello.'

"He said, 'Hello.'

"We just stood there again, then I asked him, 'What's wrong with your face?'

"He said, 'Oh — sorry. I forgot.' Then he sort of shook his head back and forth, and it looked blurry for a second, then his face got normal. He looked about the same age as me, and he had brown hair and brown eyes, and a few freckles.

"'I saw you yesterday. You're buried under the swimming pool?'

"He nodded.

"I thought about this for a moment. 'Can I still swim in it?' He nodded again and then just disappeared."

Chris looked preoccupied for a minute or two as more memories came out. "I saw that ghost again, a lot. We became friends. His name was Henry, I remember now. He told me he died in 1929; he was nineteen when he died, but he was really small for nineteen, he was about as tall as I was. He had an accent, like English or Irish, and he wore old-fashioned clothes, like his shirt had ruffles or something on the front."

Part of me was wishing this whole set of memories would go back where they came from. It was strange that I was more comfortable with the sexual abuse memories, but I didn't know what to do with this idea of seeing ghosts. The fact that I believed Chris was making me start to doubt my own hold on reality. But the important thing was that Chris believed these memories, and Chris needed me to believe him. For me, that was the real issue.

There was one precedent to Chris's experience that I was aware of, something I had read in a biography years ago. The subject of the book had been severely sexually abused by her family from early childhood. She had developed multiple personalities, which was the main topic of the book; but she had also had a friend who was a ghost. She had described him as an old man with a big moustache and bushy hair, dressed like a peasant. He would appear when she needed comforting, and was very grandfatherly and reassuring. She reported that he mentioned a dance called a "farandola," which, when the author researched it, actually turned out to be a European folk dance. The author couldn't come up with an explanation for the girl knowing this obscure word.

Chris saw Henry frequently after their first meeting. Often, when the rest of the family was out, Henry would wander into the living room and watch television with Chris. He was fascinated with the Sega Genesis, and Chris would show him how to play video games. "Henry said it was really lonely being dead. You couldn't touch anything and people wouldn't know you were there. I was the only one who had ever been able to see him."

They would hang out in his room after school. Chris would play rap music, and Henry didn't like it much; apparently, he complained that there was a lot of bad language in it. Chris told me he dressed like a rapper back then, with pants down below his hips so that his boxers stuck out and really big T-shirts to cover them. Henry laughed at that and asked why he wore his pants down with his willie sticking out. Henry could morph from one set of clothes to another. "It was cool to watch, and I used to ask him to do it. He explained that they weren't real clothes anyway, he sort of made them up. He could change his face, and sometimes he would tease me by doing the black eyes and sharp teeth, or showing up headless. He liked to freak me out, but just for a joke.

"Henry grew up on a farm around where my house was now. His father was a bad drunk, and he eventually went crazy and killed the whole family with a scythe. The headless lady that I saw sometimes was Henry's mother, but Henry wasn't able to talk to her, he didn't know why. He also didn't know why he was stuck here. But he did tell me that, since we moved in, things had started happening, like a door had opened. Our family seemed to be stirring up major shit."

Chris told me that Henry knew what Ursula was doing but he couldn't do anything about it. He once told Chris, "Be careful, my friend. She is a witch!"

Chris described seeing other ghosts too. "Once I saw a man, and he looked really scruffy, and kind of scary. I asked him who the hell he was and what he was doing, and this really deep voice said, 'Mind your tongue, boy, or I'll take off my belt to you!' Then he disappeared. He showed up every now and then, and he liked to try to scare me — but we talked sometimes. His name was Seth, and he had been a butcher. He always wore boots up to his knees, dress pants, a white shirt, and some kind of vest. He looked like he hadn't shaved or bathed in a while — not that ghosts take showers or anything."

"I kept seeing Henry until I was fourteen or fifteen, and then he passed on. He came to tell me goodbye, and I was glad for him, but I really missed him. The only person in the whole house that I could talk to had been dead for seventy years, and now he was gone and I had nobody."

Chapter Twenty-Seven

Love Is What You Go Through with Someone

Summer was coming, and Frank and I had opened our cottage for the season. It was in Waubaushene, on Georgian Bay, about ninety minutes north of Toronto. We went up on weekends with Chris and the dogs, and every other weekend we took Connor with us to give my son and daughter-in-law a break.

A waterfront cottage had been Frank's lifelong dream, and he spent every weekend puttering around on different projects. When we first bought the place, it was an old bait shop with an unfinished apartment upstairs. We spent twelve years and thousands of dollars fixing it up, and it was Frank's pride and joy. It was surrounded by a breakwall, and the water was twenty feet from the cottage in three directions; it felt like being on a cruise ship. We had a pontoon boat that could take us out to Georgian Bay on Lake Huron, and paddleboats to toodle around the inlet and explore the nearby islands. My favourite thing was going out on the upstairs balcony in the evening; the sunsets are like God's slow-motion fireworks.

The dogs loved the cottage, and Hazzard turned out to be an exceptional swimmer. He would go out in deep water and swim back and forth, like an athlete swimming laps. He could actually hold his breath underwater: Chris was looking for him one morning, and watched him surface after a dive. Nika stuck to the shallow water, where she could chase bullfrogs for hours.

Chris had been to the cottage with my youth group, and he liked being there. But now his invisible entourage was showing up as well, and the cottage had no safe place like the main floor at our house. When it was just us, I could stick close to him and head off the flashbacks. But when Connor was with us for the weekend, I sometimes felt like I needed to be triplets to keep up with everything.

Connor loved Chris to death: here was a grown-up who would play with him for hours like another kid. Chris was tremendously patient with him, and I think having Connor to focus on helped with the hallucinations. Getting to be a kid again for a while seemed to bring back the happy times from Chris's own childhood. But being around a happy three-year-old brought up some bitterness as well. "When I was his age, I was already getting the fist or the boot. Why couldn't things have been like this for me? I wish Eddie had died and it had just been my mom and Janice and me." I remembered the photo of the sombre toddler and compared it to Connor's beaming, confident personality, and I grieved for Chris.

After Connor was put to bed (a process that he milked shamelessly for extra stories, songs, and conversation), Chris would need to talk for hours. I knew that, after losing so many relationships, Chris was desperately paranoid about me liking anyone else; he had once had a pseudoseizure after seeing me casually hug a friend. He was wretchedly ashamed of being possessive, but his insecurity had been driven bone-deep, and it would take a lot of affection and reassurance to leach it out.

When we were around other people, Chris would be embarrassed by too much affection. But when it was just the two of us, he needed hugs almost constantly. He would watch television with his head in my lap. If he took a nap (and he often needed to, after sleepless nights), he wanted me to lie down next to him until he fell asleep, the way I did with Connor. I would stroke his head, and pat his back, and say, "Shhh, Shhhh," until he dozed off; his snores were deep and rushed, as if his poor brain was trying to get as much rest as it could before the nightmares showed up.

About this time, I read an article about oxytocin, a chemical released in the brain as a response to physical contact: the author called it the "cuddle chemical." It was involved in imprinting mother-child and mating bonds in animals, and it apparently reduced anxiety and blood pressure in humans. I wondered whether this was responsible for at least part of Chris's need for physical affection. I don't know if there are any medications that promote oxytocin production in the brain, but this should be explored as a treatment for anxiety disorders, and particularly PTSD. I know that the physical affection Chris got often calmed him as much as the Ativan.

Connor's playfulness had a similar effect. Chris would tutor Connor on video games, especially the old Super Mario Bros. and Spyro the Dragon games from his own childhood. Then the two of them would watch *The Dukes of Hazzard* videos, or *Teenage Mutant Ninja Turtles* movies and cartoons. They would sit in the living room all afternoon, one big couch potato and one little couch potato, discussing how many General Lee stunt cars were used, or the difference between swords and daggers as ninja weapons. Connor thought his "Uncle Chris" was cool, and Chris loved being looked up to.

The truth is that Chris had very few people in his life, and he was too nervous at the time to meet new people. My son John and his wife Sharon would invite Chris over for the weekend once or twice a month to give me a break; Chris enjoyed the change of scene, but his invisible entourage was there full-time and he didn't want people knowing that he hallucinated. He would keep himself from flashbacks by sheer will during the day, and stay awake with them all night. He enjoyed the visits, but he couldn't tolerate them very often. By the end of our second year with Chris, Sharon had a new baby, and the visits stopped.

So Chris and I were drifting into a kind of two-person twilight world together. We would both sleep in during the morning: I would get up to make coffee for my husband Frank, then go back to bed until almost noon. I would usually be up before Chris, since he often had to take Ativan to sleep, and I could get some housework done. Then I got Chris up, made sure he had his first of four sets of medication for the day, and tried to get some food or Ensure into him. We would wait for his morning vomit, hoping that the meds had been absorbed before it happened. Then we would run errands for an hour or so, which was all he could tolerate at one time. We would get home, have lunch, midday pills, Ensure, vomit; then we would take the dogs out for a walk. When we got home, Chris would nap or watch TV while I fixed supper, and he would have his third set of pills. When Frank got home, I would have supper and watch TV with him. Last set of pills and Ensure. Then Chris was ready for an evening talk session. These sessions could go on for an hour, or all night. Finally, we would fall asleep in the early morning, and the next day it would start all over again. It was the sort of life a new mother would have, taking care of her newborn child. And at that point, Chris was in many ways just as fragile and helpless.

Chapter Twenty-Eight

Daisy Duke Puts Out for PlayStation 2

The nightmares got worse, and Chris hated going to sleep at night. It took three or four Ativan to relax him enough to drift off, and he would wake up from nightmares two or three times a night, sometimes wet with sweat, sometimes crying. The paradox of these dreams was that they helped to drain the toxic memories from the subconscious, but he was being retraumatized in the process. I knew that some psychiatrists tried propranolol, a beta-adrenalin blocker, to keep this from happening; it reduced adrenalin rushes from the memories, and stopped the neurochemical process that recreates the trauma from the memory. We tried it for a while, but I think that Chris's brain was too out of control for anything to have an effect. So we just had to ride out the storm.

One nightmare in particular kept repeating for months. Chris is in a graveyard, surrounded by acres of headstones. Zombies come out from behind the headstones and chase him. Chris runs as fast as he can, but there are hundreds of them and they corner him. His feet freeze to the ground. He can't move as the zombies tear off his clothes. Then one slashes open his chest and rips out his spine. He collapses on the ground like a blob of jelly with arms and legs. A wall of mirrors appears and Chris sees himself reflected a hundred times. Then the zombies close in; they tear him to pieces and eat him. He pulls out of his body when they are doing this and watches from above as he is ripped apart and devoured. Then the dream begins all over again, in an endless loop. Sometimes his skin is torn off, sometimes his arms and legs are pulled off and he crawls to the mirror as a wriggling torso. The dream is so realistic that he can feel the damp grass under his feet and the cool air on his skin. He remembers the smells of the graveyard and the dead-meat stench of the zombies. Worst of all, he feels the pain of being torn apart, time after time.

I came up with a hypothesis for this dream. In one of my psych courses, we covered Fritz Perls's method of dream interpretation: basically, that everything in your dream is an aspect of you. I sensed that the zombies were memories: they came out of graves, like his memories, and they were destroying him in a sense. The terror he felt, and even the physical pain, which often persisted after he woke up, could have been the affective and sensory facets of the memories that he described so dispassionately during the day.

Of course, this great insight didn't tell me how to stop the dreams or help Chris deal with them. And just letting the process continue wasn't an option; as Chris himself put it, it was a really big graveyard.

The PlayStation 2 started getting a lot of use when Chris had nightmares and needed to calm down. At first, he had a really hard time concentrating and couldn't beat even simple games, which frustrated him to no end. But slowly, his concentration improved. It gave him a sense of control and accomplishment. He bought more complicated games, and was able to focus on them when he couldn't focus on anything else. It was also a way to distract himself from memories and hallucinations. It was funny to think of video games as therapy, but I was beginning to learn that help is where you find it.

I would hear him swearing at night, and get up in a panic, only to find him in front of the television with the controls in his hands, trying to beat a timed mission. He tried to find the other *Dukes of Hazzard* games, especially one that he remembered as *Daisy Duke Puts Out*. It sounded a bit X-rated for a game, but we made the rounds of the video game resale stores. One salesman at EB Games told Chris that he had a copy of *Daisy Dukes It Out*: he said that if Chris ever did come across the other game, he should come back in and the salesman would buy it off him. Chris was a bit embarrassed, but really happy with his new possession.

Chris also bought a Walkman that played CDs. He would listen to his headbanger music, cranked up as high as he could get it, and blast it through his earphones without anyone else hearing. Sometimes I would come downstairs and see him bobbing back and forth with his eyes shut and his face screwed up in concentration, lip-synching one of his songs, and I'd just watch and grin. When he noticed me, he would yelp and jump about a foot into the air; I felt bad, since I knew he was easily startled, but I had to get my humour where I could find it, too.

Chris had an encyclopedic knowledge of heavy metal music, from lyrics to band histories, and he enjoyed educating me. I grew up on Joni Mitchell and Chicago, and I seriously believed that heavy metal music was all drugs, sex, and Satanism. Chris gave me some lyrics to read from Metallica and Megadeth, and it wasn't what I'd thought at all. The songs articulated feelings of anger and pain, but weren't really that different from other styles. They just had a very primal, raw feeling; I could see why Chris related to them. You could burn off a lot of rage with this music.

Another interest that had begun to resurface made me a bit nervous: Chris loved horror movies. I've never been able to watch movies like *Nightmare on Elm Street*: I take the violence very seriously. Chris laughed at it. I guess that after living with horror in real life, the movie version seemed cartoonish. I watched a few movies with him, and he got back at me for laughing at his headbanging; I would jump and scream, and Chris just loved it. I was more fun than the movie.

Chris was really affected by the *Friday the 13th* movies. Jason, the killer in the hockey mask, used to be a deformed, mentally disabled boy who drowned when some camp counsellors weren't paying attention. His mother was killed while trying to get revenge, and this brought him back to life. Chris identified with Jason, and I realized that Chris was also getting out a lot of rage against the people who had destroyed his life; he must have fantasized about taking a machete to Eddie or Jacques hundreds of times.

The memories kept coming, but now that he had something to ground him in the present, he seemed to tolerate them better. Little glimmers of confidence began to show, even in the worst memories. And they did get worse: Jacques was a consummate sadist.

"One time, we were in the garage. They had already finished raping me. Jacques made me stand by his car, and opened the driver's door. He held my fingers against the door latch, and slammed the door. It felt like my finger was getting pulled right off my hand. It was hanging loose, like it was just connected to my hand by the skin. Then he did the same with my other fingers. He used a hammer on my toes. I thought I was crippled for life. I crawled inside and up the stairs on my knees and elbows. I got to my room and sat on the floor, just looking at my floppy fingers and crying. Then I remembered something from kindergarten: I had dislocated a finger on the playground, and my kindergarten teacher had popped it back in. I went to the bureau, and opened the drawer. I positioned the finger above the joint, inside the drawer, and slammed it shut with all my weight. It hurt like hell, but it worked — the finger was okay. I was so relieved, I was almost laughing. I did the same thing with the other fingers, it took a while, and the thumbs were the hardest because I couldn't position them right. The toes were easier now that I could use my hands; I popped the little toes in by hand, but the big toes were harder. I kept a hammer under my bed for protection, and I used it to tap the toes into the joints. I was exhausted by then, and my hands were black and swollen, so I skipped school that day and just slept in."

"Didn't your family see your hands and wonder what the hell happened?"

"Ursula would lock me in my room when I looked beat up, and tell the family that I was grounded. Sometimes she would feed me and sometimes she wouldn't, so I kept Cokes and candy bars under the bed just in case."

I found Chris's resourcefulness as incredible as I found his experiences horrifying. I had read about children who had survived abusive childhoods fairly intact; they were termed "superkids." The study comparing these children with abused peers, or even siblings who had been far more damaged by the abuse, had concluded that these children had two differences. First, they were clear about the reality of the situation: they didn't buy into the abuser's excuses or delusions. This described Chris perfectly: he was very sure about who the good guys and bad guys were. Second, the superkids had experienced a healthy, positive relationship at some point: with a grandparent, a teacher, it didn't matter. These kids had a healthy concept of love, which they could use as magnetic north to keep their bearings throughout years of abuse. Chris had his mother. He had also kept alive his memories of his relatives in northern Ontario, and remembered it as a world where bad things didn't happen. That world was his antidote to life in Ottawa.

CHAPTER TWENTY-NINE

...AND THEY BROUGHT FRIENDS

During his second summer with us, Chris spent two weeks with his Aunt Claire and Uncle Pierre at their trailer park near Astorville. Besides being a chance to spend time with his mother's family, it was a respite from his symptoms. For some reason, he didn't hallucinate or have attacks of vomiting when he visited his mother's relatives. He could actually see Jacques and Ursula at the airport entrance, banging on the doors and trying to get past some invisible barrier his mind created for them. It was a great send-off.

"My aunt and I spent a lot of time talking. She can read lips, and when that doesn't work I write things down. I started remembering a bit of my French while I was up there. My aunt wears dentures, and it's so cute when she's talking French with her teeth out. It's kind of hard to understand, but I love it.

"Uncle Pierre and I sat around and had beers together. They have a little vegetable garden out back. We visited the neighbours or took a ride into town for supplies. At night, we had a bonfire and ate supper. It was really quiet, no TV or anything, so we just sat around and talked."

The two weeks with his aunt and uncle were very reassuring to Chris. He brought home a pile of photographs, and he looked at them constantly — he even slept with them by his bed. And he was right about his French: it was beginning to come back. He tried to teach me some words, and had a great time teasing me about my lousy pronunciation. I told him that it all sounded like "gargle and hawk" to me.

By this time, I had picked up on a pattern of memory recovery: when something good happened and Chris felt happy, he built up a reserve of energy. Then he would start to get irritable, and his vomiting and nightmares would get worse. Graves would start opening in his memory graveyard. Finally, he would go into a crisis and the memories would pour out.

This time was a bit different. In addition to the other symptoms, Chris began to see a new group of hallucinations. At first, they were human outlines full of static. As they filled in and developed features, Chris began to remember his other abusers: Jim and Dave.

"Ursula used to take me over to Jacques's house sometimes. There was about an acre of bush around it. He had a big garage next to the house, he worked out of there as a mechanic. I remember him putting me in this pit in the floor, it was full of filthy water, then he put this grate over the top. I was crouched down in there for an hour, the water was really cold and there was this dead rat floating around in it." (I asked my husband, who is a mechanic, why a pit like that would be in a garage. He explained that it was a drain for washing oil off the floor after fixing cars. He didn't ask why I wanted to know; I had learned by now that he couldn't take hearing about Chris's memories.)

"Jacques liked to cook, and Ursula used to take me over for supper. I would sit in the kitchen while they fixed the food. Jacques would jerk off and mix the sperm in with my food, then he made me eat it. I think that's when I started throwing up after eating. I still do that, I can't help it. And I can't eat anything with cream sauce, it's even hard to drink milk because of the texture.

"One time we went to Jacques's house and there were two other guys there. I got a really bad feeling about that. Jacques introduced them as Jim and Dave. Jacques made me take my clothes off and stand in the kitchen while they were all having supper. Afterwards, they brought me upstairs to the bedroom and took turns with me.

"Jim and Dave were long-distance truckers who were buddies of Jacques; they were also into drug-dealing. Dave was this scrawny, creepy guy who kind of looked like the actor Willem Dafoe. He lived with his two brothers, Freddie and Michael. I got to meet them, too.

"Jim was a big, red-headed Irishman who came from the States. He had been in the Marines a long time ago, he was probably in his forties. He had a Marine tattoo on his arm. He liked to work out, and he would take me to the gym with him and teach me how to use the equipment. It was kind of creepy, this guy being all buddy-buddy one day, and raping me the next.

"Now when I went over to Jacques's house, Jim and Dave would be there, too. Besides raping me, they liked to beat me up. One time, they tied me to a chair and Jim kept throwing a baseball at me. He had a really good arm; I had these round bruises all over my legs and chest for a week. Jacques would use me for target practice: he would put me against a wall and shoot at me. He had a whole collection of guns, but the one he liked best was an Uzi machine gun. He wouldn't hit me, but there were all these mason jars on the shelves and I would get cuts from the shattering glass."

Now there were four hallucinations following Chris around everywhere. This wasn't as bad as the memories that kept popping out; it was as if we were back at the first few weeks after he had remembered the original abuse by Ursula. It seemed strange how the memories came out in groups, like they were stored in separate little time capsules inside Chris's head. Once a time capsule was opened, some memories just came out automatically. Others seemed to come out in dreams; after Chris talked about a new nightmare, the memory behind it would materialize. Or they surfaced as "phantom pains," our term for sensory flashbacks of pain: Chris would feel as if someone had kicked him, and then remember an incident in which he was actually kicked. Still others were triggered by everyday items or activities, which turned each day into a walk through a minefield. I remember one quiet afternoon when Chris was watching the movie *Casino*. He saw the scene where the cheating gambler got zapped, and told me, "Hey, that's a cattle prod. Boy, those things can make you pray for a heart attack." And we were off on about an hour of new memories.

Chris would start off absolutely driven to tell the memory. At that point, I just listened and maybe asked a question if his narrative became confused, which it often did: sometimes his thoughts came out like a pile of junk pouring out of a closet when a sitcom character opens the door. After he slowed down, we would go back over the memory and talk it over, draining the emotional affect it had brought with it. When Chris started to lose interest in the topic and go on to other things, I knew we were done.

I know that this sounds like an amateur therapy session, and it probably was. But it was therapy on demand, day or night, at the moment it was needed, and I think that increased the impact on his healing. It reminded me of an anecdote that I had read in James Herriot's *All Creatures Great and Small*: Dr. Herriot had seen a poor farmer's only milk cow, which had developed a serious udder infection. Dr. Herriot told the man that it was pretty hopeless, but he might try milking the cow periodically to clean the pus out. The next day, the veterinarian returned and was shocked to find the cow practically cured. The farmer, on the other hand, was exhausted: he had taken the advice seriously, and had stayed up all night milking the cow to keep the udder cleared out. Sometimes that is what it takes to heal things.

When we weren't in therapy mode, the other important strategy was distraction. Comedy movies were really helpful, for both of us; Chris introduced me to Mr. Bean. (A word to the wise: never watch the Christmas turkey episode on a full bladder. I'm not kidding.) A second option was blowing off steam: action movies were great for this, especially if they had jokes in them as well as stuff blowing up.

Getting out of the house was really important, although we could only manage it for short periods before Chris would start to have flashbacks. Taking the dogs out was our most successful kind of outing. There were acres of fields near our house, with a creek winding through. Hazzard loved the creek, especially the deep parts: he would swim laps for half an hour without a break, as if he were training for the Olympics. Then he would chase the ducks that nested along the banks; they would fly low to lead him away, and he loved the chase. And Chris was as proud of Hazzard's athletic ability as any hockey dad. It gave him something to talk about with the other dog owners — Chris was good at starting conversations with people at the dog park, and he remembered names and details about their dogs; he was polite, outgoing, and had a remarkable ability to connect with people. That was almost the only time he would talk to strangers; even his stammer didn't stop him. So, even though it set off his anxiety, Chris really needed to be around people. It was a frustrating situation.

CHAPTER THIRTY

REZONING THE GRAVEYARD

By the autumn of our second year, Chris started getting really irritable in the evenings. More coffins started coming out of the ground in the memory graveyard, but these looked different. They were metal, and had chains around them to keep the memories inside. They glowed with heat; the cracks showed molten orange, and the stinging odour of burning iron hung over the tombstones. The idea of these coffins opening terrified Chris.

The first memory lived up to its introduction. It was a whole new level of horror.

It happened during one of our nightly talks in the living room. Chris would sit on the loveseat, and I would sit near him on the end of the sofa. That night, we visualized opening one of the coffins; Chris felt ready to tackle it. He described in detail how he was prying the lid off, and the black fog that slid out and engulfed him. Then he closed his eyes and concentrated as the memory coalesced in his head.

"Jim and Dave were drug dealers. Dave kept telling Jacques that they should kill me so I couldn't tell on them. But Jacques said if *he* wanted to kill me, he would. I was *his* toy. Ursula used to call me her fucking-doll. By that time, I didn't feel human anyway, but it was creepy to be talked about like I was just a thing. It felt like every day might be my last.

"One day, I was down in Dave's basement, tied to a chair, all bloody, and my clothes were ripped. It was after one of the sessions. This girl came downstairs to talk to Dave, she looked at me and then looked away, I felt really ashamed. She went into the other room with Dave. I heard the others talking about her, saying that she was one of Dave's dealers and she had come up short a few times, he was pretty mad about it. Suddenly I heard screaming coming from the room, and a gunshot. Then it was really quiet, even Jim and Jacques shut up. Dave came out and told Jim to get the chainsaw and some bags. They were in the room for a while, and then Jim dragged out some black garbage bags. He carried them up the stairs. They took a gallon of bleach and a bucket of water into the room, and they were there for a while again. I could smell the bleach from where I was, so it must have been intense in the room. Finally, Dave came out and noticed me still tied to the chair. I think that's when he had the conversation with Jacques about killing me."

Chris was exhausted by this memory, and I was really frightened for the first time. Sexual abuse is a crime, but it is so rarely prosecuted that the legal system was the least of our issues. Chris wasn't ready to go to the police and, like most victims, didn't expect them to believe him anyway. But witnessing a murder was a whole other situation.

I knocked Chris out with Ativan and stayed up the rest of the night worrying. There was the possibility that this memory wasn't accurate, but that was a faint hope. Chris had described the scene as accurately as he did with his rape sessions, and with the same dispassionate tone. I considered going to the police. Then I pictured myself telling them that my mentally ill boarder had recovered a memory of a murder, ten years earlier, in another city, of an unnamed girl by a drug dealer named Dave. The worst that could happen was Chris getting involved with a police investigation, and possibly facing some kind of charges. The likeliest scenario was him being treated like a lunatic by some desk sergeant. And I knew how anxious the police were to avoid getting involved in "historic" child abuse cases (their term for a case reported by the adult victim years after the fact). I had already tried to involve them when Chris's memories first started coming out. I was bounced back and forth between Mississauga and Ottawa, each police department saying it was the other's jurisdiction, until I gave up. Until Chris could come up with something more concrete, it was useless to go to the police. I was tremendously relieved by this decision, until I remembered all the other glowing coffins in that goddamned graveyard.

And then, just when I didn't think things could get any worse, a "super-coffin" appeared in the graveyard. It was enormous and glowing, and covered with skulls and pentagrams. The chains around it were extra thick, and the padlock was huge. This coffin vibrated as if something were trying to kick its way out. Chris was incapacitated with terror: he couldn't think of anything else. Considering the memories that had already come out, I couldn't even imagine what could be in that monster casket. The only possibilities I could come up with were thermonuclear war or the ten plagues of Egypt.

Finally, I decided to ask Chris if his last set of memories might be hallucinations. I was reluctant to suggest it. Chris was terrified of not being believed, and if I could discount *these* memories, what about all the other memories that he had recovered?

Surprisingly, Chris jumped on the possibility that the memories weren't real. He was actually quite enthusiastic about it, which made me suspicious. He was desperate for them to be hallucinations. That would have been my reaction to having an experience like that, and, paradoxically, it was the best indication that the memories were accurate, like it or not. It was also an indication that Chris had dug up something that he wasn't ready to deal with.

In late October, Chris solved the problem himself. One morning he told me that his graveyard was empty. All the tombstones were gone — even the monster coffin had vanished. As far as he was concerned, there were no more memories to unearth. I was suspicious of this new development, but I figured that Chris's subconscious mind had decided to give him a much-needed vacation from his traumatic past. It was a welcome relief for both of us. For the next three years, there were small recovered memories that were related to experiences that Chris had already remembered. But the reburied memories never showed up again during that time.

CHAPTER THIRTY-ONE

"GOODBYE, MY SON"

By spring of our second year, Hazzard was almost a year old. He was taller than Nika, but leaner and more loose-limbed. He was a grab bag of breed characteristics, but there had to be some hound in him: he was a natural hunter. He was as fast as a greyhound, swam better than a retriever, and had a mouthful of teeth that looked like a beartrap. He wasn't meant to be a house dog; if we didn't walk him twice a day, he started to go stir-crazy. Chris began to take him around the block on his own now. Focusing on Hazzard helped him avoid the hallucinations for short periods.

Chris loved having Hazzard, but the day-to-day responsibilities of caring for a dog were too much for him sometimes. I ended up with another mouth to feed and one more backside to worry about. And Hazzard regarded his bathroom breaks as an opportunity to tour the neighbourhood. He had a mind of his own, and when he decided to take off, there was no way to outrun him. And he didn't leave delicate little poops on the neighbours' lawns: it looked like a small horse had been there.

I also learned not to yell at Hazzard, or punish him in any way, in front of Chris. It brought back memories of his other dogs:

"When my mom died, my dad got us a dog. She was part beagle, and we named her Precious. She used to go to the bathroom on the floor sometimes, and my dad would beat her. I would hear her crying for ten minutes sometimes, and it made me really mad. Nobody was bothering to housebreak her, or take her out so she would learn to go outside. I tried to teach her, but I was at school a lot of the time and it wasn't enough. Eddie was such an asshole. We didn't have Precious for very long.

"Later we had a dog named Sasha. She was a lot bigger than Precious, she was part wolfhound or something. She was more house-trained than Precious, but she would still have accidents and Ursula would beat her too. I would get mad at that and tell Ursula to take her outside more often, but then she'd start yelling at me. I would take Sasha for walks; she was a really sweet dog, and she was just about the only one in the house I could stand. We had her for two or three years, but I don't remember what happened to her either."

Hazzard was smart when he wanted to be: he learned to open latched doors. If we left the back door open, he could press down the latch on the screen door and get out. Nika took a more direct route; she simply went through the screen. We had replaced every screen in our house and cottage at some point. Now we had grilles on the screen doors to keep her in, but we had to keep our doors shut to stop Hazzard from escaping.

One night, some of the neighbour children knocked on our door to ask if Hazzard was there. He didn't come when I called, and I noticed the back door was open and the screen door unlatched. I went back to the front, thinking Hazzard must be out terrorizing the neighbourhood. The oldest girl told me that they had been walking home and had seen a dog hit by a car on the main street behind our house. It looked like Hazzard, who was pretty well-known around the neighbourhood, but they wanted to be sure before they said anything. My heart fell like a stone into my stomach. I asked the girls where they had seen the dog, and ran the two blocks to the main street.

He was lying in the street next to the curb. I knelt down beside the body: it was beginning to cool, and the muscles were limp. He was definitely gone. There was no blood; the car must have broken his neck and killed him instantly. I thanked God that I could tell Chris that much — and then cussed Him up one side and down the other for letting this happen. Chris had so much to deal with already, I didn't know what this was going to do to him.

I picked Hazzard up in my arms; the body felt cold, loose, and empty after all that energy. I carried him back up the lane to the backyard. I was numb, except for my fear of how Chris was going to react; this was going to be a major meltdown. I laid the body down behind the shed at the back of the yard. I didn't want Chris to see him before he was ready. I stayed for a few minutes to say goodbye; then I gathered myself to break the news to Chris.

He had heard what the neighbour kids had said, and when he saw my face he figured it out. He seemed remarkably calm. I sat down with him on the living room sofa. "Honey, Hazzard is gone. From what I can tell, it was really quick, he didn't suffer or anything. I brought him home. He's in the backyard now. Do you want to go out and see him? I can go with you."

Chris shook his head violently. "No, I don't want to look at him like that." He sat for a few minutes. "Mom, later on, can I get another dog?"

I knew that Chris loved Hazzard, and he had trouble expressing feelings, but it was hard to believe that he was already thinking about replacing him.

"Honey, if you're up to having another dog, we can get another dog. Are you okay?"

"Yes, I'm just going to go downstairs for a while and listen to my music, okay?"

On one level, I was relieved that Chris wasn't having a psychotic break. On another, his calmness made me nervous. I went down to check on him; he had his headphones on, and he was rocking back and forth to the music with his eyes shut and his lips moving silently. Photographs of Hazzard were all over the bed. I went back upstairs; if there was one thing Chris knew how to do, it was deal with disasters.

I buried Hazzard in the back garden, under the plum tree. I covered the grave with stones, then I told Chris that it was all done. He went outside and sat by the grave for a little while. When he came in, he started talking about some new memories that had nothing to do with Hazzard. It was as if he had buried his grief as quickly as he used to bury his traumatic experiences. Maybe he just didn't have the energy to grieve.

A few nights later, around two in the morning, I got up for a trip to the bathroom. I heard Chris in the kitchen, talking to himself. This wasn't unusual; Chris would often talk in a soft, stammering voice when he was alone. As I listened, I could hear that, this time, he wasn't talking to himself:

"Good-good-g-goodbye, Hazzard. Goo-g-goodbye, my son. Goo-g-good-goodbye. Daddy ... daddy ... lov-loves you and and and miss-misses you very much. Da-d-daddy loves y-you…"

I went quietly back to bed.

CHAPTER THIRTY-TWO

STARTING TO FIGHT BACK

The months after Hazzard's death were uneventful. Chris was still housebound, vomiting, and hallucinating. He seemed to be at a plateau in the healing process, though; there weren't any new memories or symptoms, which was a relief for both of us.

I was noticing that Chris seemed to have layers of emotions. The top layer, where he lived most of the time, was an atmosphere of fear. Any change in the house, our schedule, even the wrong word or look from me, would set off a simmering panic that would last for days. It would take hours of talk to get to the problem, especially if it was something he thought would upset me. Breaking a glass or eating the last of the ice cream was like committing a crime: and he would play it out like a character from a Dostoevsky novel, hiding his terrible guilt, brooding about being discovered, finally confessing and expecting to be thrown out in the snow and eaten by Siberian wolves. It would be funny if he weren't so absolutely serious about it. No matter how many reassurances I gave him, they would wash away like a sand castle at high tide.

Under the fear was a mixture of confusion and outrage. It was directed almost exclusively at Dan and Denise, and later at Barbara as well. Every night, we would rehash every mean, greedy, cruel thing that they had ever done to him: "One night I bought a Wendy's chicken sandwich and ate it up in my room. Denise found the wrapper and yelled at me; we weren't allowed food up in our bedrooms…"

"Another time I came down for breakfast and sat in Dan's chair. Denise chewed me out for half an hour…"

It seemed so weird to me that, after the horrors he had uncovered in his past, he was so fixated on these relatively minor annoyances. Now, he rarely mentioned the sexual abuse, and was reluctant to discuss Ursula or Jacques. I figured that he needed to practice on Dan and Denise before tackling the major issues.

Under the layer of controlled outrage there seemed to be a more elemental anger — but this was still buried too deep to reach most of the time. Even in his dreams, Chris would feel fear most of the time. Only occasionally would outrage break through:

"I dreamed I was murdered by Dan and Denise, and they got away with it. I got buried, but some aliens came along and dug me up. They took me on their spaceship and regenerated me. I was taller, and built like Arnold Schwarzenegger. I went back to earth and looked for Dan and Denise. They were on trial for my murder. I sat in the court, and nobody knew who I was. Denise was on the stand, and she was telling everybody how much trouble I was and how she just took me in to be a Christian. Then I stood up and said, 'Recognize me, Denise? I'M BACK!' I sounded just like the Terminator. Denise knew who I was, and she begged for me to forgive her. I told her to go to hell, and the judge sentenced her to life in prison. Then I went out and got a job, and got married to Pamela Anderson. That was a cool dream."

Chris began to have variations of this dream a lot, and I was encouraged by it. For once, it wasn't a nightmare, and the dream themes of healing up and getting justice for his abuse were major improvements.

Occasionally, Chris would get angry; usually, he would be frustrated at his illness or the hallucinations taunting him. I got him to hit pillows or punch the sofa, and sometimes it helped. Once, he became absolutely furious at a letter he had found in his belongings, from his Aunt Olga to Barbara, describing how to take care of him as if he were some kind of mental defective who couldn't even dress himself. He was angrier than I had seen him in months. I suggested burning the letter, which thrilled him: we lit it on fire and burned it in the laundry sink while Chris did a spontaneous war dance around the laundry room. It was a very cathartic experience; after that, every time he found a letter or photo that upset him, we burned it at the stake.

Chapter Thirty-Three

I'm with the Band

Chris had been living with us for just over two years by now, and we decided to celebrate December 12 as the anniversary of our mutual adoption, and we've celebrated it every year since. We went out to lunch together, and bought each other cards. The first Adoption Day meant a great deal to Chris, confirming the bond between us, and I enjoyed it too.

After Adoption Day, I checked with his mother's relatives up north about Christmas plans. Aunt Babette was having her house renovated, so she couldn't have Chris up for a visit. But Uncle Pierre and Aunt Claire asked him up for a week, and he was thrilled. Again, we bought presents for every living being in the town, and Chris gave me the rundown on his family background for two generations back. I couldn't believe how much these people mattered to him, and deep down I prayed they were worth his adoration.

I waited with Chris at the station till the Northlander train boarded; it was a ten-hour trip, which worried me. We didn't have cellphones then, so I taught Chris to call collect at the stops and let me know he was okay. His hallucinations stayed behind again, which both relieved and fascinated me.

Christmas at home was unusually quiet; we had the usual visits with relatives, and my son's family came on Boxing Day, but I was exhausted. I hadn't realized how difficult it was to care for Chris until I had a week off. Now, I'd had families on my caseload that had cared for disabled members their whole lives; I could manage as long as I needed to, and I figured the worst was over. But I had to admit that I welcomed the time off when I had the chance.

Chris returned home for New Year's relaxed and cheerful. He was pretty full of energy, so I thought we might try something new to get him out in the world a bit. He had decided to learn the guitar, so his late Christmas present was a new electric guitar. We went to some of the big music stores in town, but we ended up at a small music shop we happened across in a nearby mall, ambitiously named Guitar World. Chris spent some time checking out guitars and struck up a conversation with the owner, Jim, about heavy metal music. He seemed really comfortable in this friendly little shop, and Jim helped him pick out a good starter guitar, a Flying V like James Hetfield of Metallica, and knocked twenty dollars off the price. I noticed that Guitar World also offered lessons, so I crossed my fingers and signed him up for half an hour per week.

The first lesson went better than I expected. I stayed in the store while Chris had his private class in the back area, and talked with Jim. He was an ex-musician who knew a lot about instruments, and this was his first try at his own business. I mentioned casually that Chris might need a bit of extra help because of his disability; Jim shrugged and said that he hadn't noticed any problems.

Chris got through the whole lesson without any anxiety attacks or flashbacks. He even stuck around for a while and talked music with Jim. I stood back and watched: Chris looked almost normal, except for the stutter, and Jim was taking it in stride. By the time we left, Chris was in love with Guitar World. He started looking forward to his guitar lessons; and I was so glad that Chris finally *had* something to look forward to that I would have paid any price for those lessons.

Guitar World became the only place other than our house where Chris didn't have hallucinations. He would hang out there after the lessons and check out guitars. He struck up friendships with Dave, the store clerk who was his age and starting up a band, and with Stringer, the craftsman who built and repaired guitars on-site. I was actually able to leave him there for half an hour and shop or go for coffee. I started looking forward to the lessons almost as much as Chris did.

The guitar started showing up in Chris's dreams, the first really happy ones he'd had since his breakdown. He dreamed that he joined a rock band and became the lead guitarist. He became rich and famous, and when his dad's relatives came and saw him at a concert, they were shocked. He'd sneer at them from the stage and say, "What's the matter? I thought I was supposed to be the handicapped kid who couldn't do anything! Look at me now; I guess you were wrong, eh?" They'd slink away while the crowd roared.

Around this time, I ran into one of my old clients, Bobby, who was working at a video store. He was a friendly guy who had a mild intellectual disability, a habit of hugging everybody, and a gift for drumming. When I was working with him, I spent a lot of time trying to find him opportunities to play music; several of the support workers I found for him were musicians themselves. But nothing ever seemed to develop for him, and that had always frustrated me.

Bobby had funding to hire a support person, but his current caseworker hadn't found anyone. I came up with a brainstorm: I could find places for Bobby to play drums, take him to the venues myself, and bring Chris along for the outings.

I phoned Bobby's mom, Jayne, and made the offer. She invited me over for coffee, and I took Chris along to introduce him. The guys started talking music, and Bobby invited Chris to his studio in the basement to show off his drum kit. Jayne and I caught up on old times and then discussed my proposal. We decided that I would start taking Chris and Bobby out together to get them used to each other. Meanwhile, I could research opportunities for Bobby to play with other musicians.

Chris was amazed at Bobby's talent with the drums, and couldn't wait to get better on his guitar so that he could play with him. This gave me an idea: where do music students go to play with other musicians? During Chris's next lesson at Guitar World, I picked Jim's brain for ideas, and learned about jam sessions. Local bars would sometimes host weekly events where musicians could get up and play with the band. There was one starting up at the Black Cat Tavern nearby, on Friday evenings.

Meanwhile, Chris and Bobby were getting along well; Bobby loved hard rock bands, and they checked out each other's CD and DVD collections for hours. Bobby was also the most sociable person I had ever met, which worked well for Chris. The only problem was that Bobby wanted a lot of my attention, and loved to hug me; this drove Chris around the bend. I spent an hour or more after every outing just reassuring Chris that I loved him as a son, and Bobby was only a friend. This would bring up old memories of rejection during the time with Ursula. It sometimes seemed that Chris had a bottomless hole inside him, and no amount of assurance would be enough to make him feel safe in a relationship.

We all headed up to the Black Cat Tavern one Friday night. I was more nervous than Bobby was; for some reason, I was picturing an audience of two or three hundred. The other thing that worried me was the possibility that they wouldn't let Bobby play because of his disability, which was pretty visible. I was used to pushing situations for my clients, but this was new territory.

I needn't have worried. The Tavern was nearly empty. The bandleader was more than willing to have Bobby jam with them, and was impressed with his ability. They played some classic rock, and even jazz, and Bobby kept up effortlessly. We even got to hang out with the band on breaks, and Chris found out that the guitarist was a fellow Francophone from Montreal. The whole evening was pure gold.

We got some leads on other jams, and soon Bobby was out two or three nights a week playing music with different bands. He was remarkably confident, and would get up onstage and play anything with anybody. He couldn't read music, but he could play a song after hearing it once. He had a huge repertoire, and what he didn't know he could fake.

Chris enjoyed the jams as well. He would sit back and listen, drink a few beers, and just be a guy for a while. The beers relaxed him, which was no surprise, and being able to drink them was important to him. "When I was eighteen, Janice and I were visiting at my grandfather's house and I wasn't allowed to drink. They would have wine with meals, even Janice, and I would get Coke or something. I remember one time when they said that alcohol wasn't good for me. Janice was sitting there with a glass in her hand. I guess nobody was worried about her health."

Bobby came from a musical family. When he was five years old, he started playing on his big brother's drum kit. When they tried to stop him by hiding the drumsticks, he would use anything available, including screwdrivers. After he had punctured a few drumheads, the family decided to buy him his own kit. Once they realized that he had real talent, his parents paid for drum lessons. He even went to a summer music camp in New Hampshire.

Two of his brothers had been professional musicians, and we kept running into people at the jam sessions who knew his family. One of them, Rafael, was in a band that played gigs at nearby bars. We started going to their performances and became friends with the other band members. We became their "groupies."

The band, Genetic Disorder, played heavy metal music. Chris was in his element. I had learned from my experience as a caseworker that disabled people's interests are their best entry into the mainstream world. They give them something in common with "normal" people who have the same interests, and promote acceptance. Chris could hold his own in any conversation about heavy metal, and probably knew more about its history than most musicians. He would buy CDs and T-shirts from the different bands at the gigs and discuss their musical influences. It made him feel normal.

CHAPTER THIRTY-FOUR

NOT ALL MARRIAGES MAKE GOOD COUNTRY SONGS

Music was also helping Chris heal. The rock band dreams started happening every night, and they were a strong antidote to the nightmares. This was the most difficult period, I think, because Chris seemed to have hit a plateau — he wasn't getting better and he wasn't getting worse: he just stayed stuck for about four months. The hallucinations were still devastating. Ursula, Jacques, Jim, and Dave were everywhere. Chris saw and heard them constantly. And they were starting to tell Chris to kill himself. He wasn't about to do it — he had gotten well enough for that — but hearing it all the time really played on his nerves.

Besides his entourage, Chris was still contending with his ongoing vomiting, his nightmares, and the mood swings that had him irritable one minute and terrified the next. He seemed to be drowning in emotions, after years of feeling almost nothing. He sometimes felt like he was crawling through his life from one moment to the next, just trying to survive.

Every two weeks, Chris would spend a day or two with my son and his family; on alternate weekends, I took care of my grandson Connor. On his weekends out, Chris enjoyed the change of scene and the chance to talk to people his age, and I had a rest and a chance to spend time with Frank. But the weekends with Connor sometimes felt like an endurance trial. Chris and Connor enjoyed spending time together, but when Connor wanted my attention, so did Chris, and vice versa. Then Frank would want something at the same time, and my brain would feel like it was going to explode.

At about this time, Frank's diabetes flared up and began to affect his eyes. Several years earlier, he had developed diabetic retinopathy: in his case, the capillaries in his retina were breaking and bleeding into the fluid behind the eye. It had caused near-total blindness for about two months until it gradually cleared up. Now, small bleeds were happening again and were starting to affect his vision. He was worried, and this made him really hard to live with. Frank preferred being mad to being scared, and he began to get upset at the time I was spending with Chris. We had frequent arguments about it, which Chris heard despite my best efforts. After each fight with my husband, I had to spend hours reassuring Chris that he wasn't going to be thrown out of the house.

When I took Chris in, I had gone into the situation with my eyes open: I had spent thirteen years listening to families with disabled members at home. They faced terrible situations that placed strains on marriages, children, and relatives. Sometimes everyone pulled together and shared the burden; other times, marriages ended, mothers had to choose between the disabled child and the other children, or relatives stopped visiting or inviting them to family functions. I also knew that Frank hadn't wanted to get this involved; he had expected Chris to get placed in a group home or something within a few months. Having a permanent member of the household with a crippling mental illness was more than he had bargained for, and it wasn't unreasonable of him to blame me for it. And it was putting a desperate strain on our relationship. I felt an increasing pressure to choose between Chris and my marriage.

Inevitably, the situation snapped. Frank and I had our worst argument in over twenty years, and I packed Chris up and walked out. We went to my son's apartment and spent the night in the spare bedroom.

Chris handled the crisis amazingly well, which surprised me — I was expecting a meltdown. I think he had been deeply affected by the fact that, in a sense, I had chosen him over my marriage. If this didn't prove that I wouldn't abandon him, nothing would.

I was dealing with some abandonment issues of my own at that moment. Unknown to me, my son and daughter-in-law had been having some serious marital problems themselves, which they had been trying to keep from Frank and me. My staying there, even for a few days, was not a welcome idea. They suggested that I would be better off at the cottage.

That night, while Chris snored away in his bed across the room, I lay awake in mine feeling abandoned by everyone I had ever counted on. It was one of the worst nights of my life. Strangely, it never occurred to me to abandon Chris: all my plans were for how to take care of the two of us at the cottage, or wherever we ended up. I'm not sure how much sense that made, but somehow it seemed that, come hell or high water, I couldn't betray someone who had so completely put his life in my hands. If Chris could survive all the things that had happened to him, who was I to wimp out over my own problems? I was ready to tell the world to kiss my ass.

I am a believer in synchronicity, C. G. Jung's concept of meaningful coincidence that reveals a purpose within events.

He described it primarily as a beneficent force; but I think that there's a dark side to it, a "reverse synchronicity," that acts destructively on situations that are already bad. Some people call it Murphy's Law. When I was a caseworker, I called it the Gypsy Curse. For some families, nothing worked out, to the point of it being ridiculous. I remember one family who took years, literally, to get a service for their son. Finally, they had a case conference set up to arrange for this service — and it was cancelled by a freak snowstorm. The storm was in late May, and was the latest on record. Now *that* is a Gypsy Curse.

But things seemed to get to their worst point just before they got better, as if the Gypsy Curse threw everything it had at a situation just before it lost its power — the family got their case conference two weeks later, and the problem that had been destroying their son's life was resolved within a month.

That night, it really seemed that the universe was throwing everything it had at me, trying to get me to give up. The next morning, I woke up with an inexplicable sense of relief. Chris and I went back to the house to pack up for the cottage. I phoned Frank at work to tell him where we would be, and we started talking. I waited for him to come home, and we talked some more. The anger that had been there for weeks wasn't gone, but the fever had drained out of it. That may have just been us coming to our senses, but I got the feeling that my decision to stay with Chris broke the back of our Gypsy Curse.

Or so I thought. A few weeks after the argument, Frank got severe retinal bleeding in both eyes. He was almost completely blind. We went to the eye specialist, who told Frank that the bleeds might clear on their own within a few months. Otherwise, he would need surgery on both eyes. You just can't keep a good Gypsy Curse down.

Frank was home from work for eight weeks. One day, while I was cutting his toenails, I noticed an abscess on his big toe. This can be dangerous for someone with diabetes, but Frank just couldn't deal with both issues at once. Since he couldn't see or feel the abscess, he wouldn't take it seriously.

Chris was looking forward to spending the holidays with his relatives again. Then a letter came from his Aunt Claire and Uncle Pierre, telling him that they were doing repairs to their house and couldn't have him up that Christmas. Although they promised to see him the next summer at the trailer, he was terribly disappointed. All things considered, it was shaping up to be a miserable Christmas.

I have learned through experience that any situation becomes "normal" if it goes on long enough. Our grandchildren threw Frank a surprise birthday party — and everything was a surprise because he couldn't see it and they had to tell him about it. Chris started looking forward to his first Christmas with his new family. We went Christmas shopping for his new nephews, and decorated the house, and set up the Christmas tree. He still missed his relatives up north, but he began to feel more like part of our family.

In late November, Frank's big toe had swollen up and turned a dark red. I knew something was wrong, but Frank still wouldn't bother with it. He was too upset about his eyes. And he thought nothing was wrong until a doctor said it was, and not going to the doctor meant you couldn't be told something was wrong. But when the toe started draining, I practically dragged him by his hair into the doctor's office. Sure enough, it was seriously infected. Frank was admitted to the hospital, still blind and now facing the amputation of his toe.

For the next few days, that toe was subjected to an amazing array of medical scrutinies — X-rays, MRIs, and a dozen specialists. You would have thought it was a vital organ. Frank went home with an intravenous pump for antibiotics, and nurses came in every day to check the pump and change his dressing. Frank couldn't stand being helpless, and he was more depressed than I had ever seen him. He even started talking about suicide, which scared me; he took insulin three times a day, and an overdose would be the simplest thing in the world. All I could do was to keep reminding him that things were going to get better, but at the time even I wasn't too sure.

A few weeks before Christmas, Frank had surgery on one eye. I had never seen my cranky, perennially pessimistic husband so grateful. After such a grim period in our marriage, Christmas was a poignantly happy time. Frank watched us opening gifts with a beatific smile on his stolid face, and laughed as he opened Connor's card and dollar-store presents. We went to Frank's sister's home for a big Italian Christmas dinner, and the whole family was congratulating him on being able to see again. Frank walked around that night like he owned the world.

Three weeks after Christmas, we got the news: the toe would have to be amputated. Despite the best efforts of the doctors, the bone infection wasn't going away. Three doctors stood at the end of Frank's hospital bed to give him the news.

Frank was in shock: he lay on the bed looking out of the window, and tears were streaming down his cheeks. I had been the one keeping up his hopes for the past three months, but now he needed to face reality.

"Frank, this isn't the end of the world. You're going to be able to walk. It isn't even going to make you limp."

"They're going to cut my toe off!"

"Frank, it's a *fucking toe!*" He looked at me in surprise; so did the doctors, who were now about two beds away talking to another patient.

I said, quietly but sternly, "You got yourself into this situation by being pigheaded. You're going to lose a toe. You're lucky that's all you're losing, and you know it. Now tell the doctors to schedule the operation!"

This pulled him out of his moment of self-pity. I knew my husband: what he needed was a way to be back in charge of the situation. He called the doctors back over, asked questions about the operation, and found out that it was only a day surgery. They scheduled it for two days later, and Frank was almost cheerful in the day-surgery waiting room. The whole thing took two hours.

At about the same time, Frank had surgery on his other eye, and that went well too. Three weeks later, he was back to work. He had war stories to tell his buddies, and they started talking about their own operations, like a bunch of teenage boys trying to outdo each other in gory details.

Going through Frank's health crisis didn't solve the whole situation with our marriage; he still resented not having a choice about Chris living with us, and deep down he was still jealous of the attention Chris got from me. But some things did change. He started treating Chris as a member of the family, and even let him call him "Dad." Chris was thrilled. And Frank was less cranky with me — not a lot, that would probably take a lobotomy, but enough to keep things going between us. I guess not all relationships make great country-music love songs; you just learn to live with what you've got. That's the secret of a good marriage.

Chapter Thirty-Five

Chris's New Puppy

By now, Chris had been hallucinating on a daily basis for almost a year, and it was the most debilitating of his symptoms. He couldn't sleep downstairs in his own room or go out of the house by himself because the images of his abusers would gang up on him, crowding in and yelling at him, telling him to give up and kill himself. They were even able to cause physical pain: when Chris hallucinated one of his abusers hitting, kicking, or strangling him, there was a corresponding sensory flashback. We called these sensations "phantom pains." The excruciating pain seemed to recede only when Chris was able to identify and talk out the memory that was causing it.

"Mom, I've got a real bad feeling in my throat. It feels like someone is strangling me."

"Okay, focus: can you remember feeling this before?"

"It feels like a hand around my throat. Jacques used to strangle me until I blacked out."

"Tell me more about the memory."

"When I fought back, Jacques would punish me by strangling me sometimes. I would get so mad at him, it wouldn't matter, though. I remember punching him in his fat gut so hard that it knocked the wind out of him."

"How's your throat?"

"Still sore, but it's getting better."

As the hallucinations hung around, the incidents of phantom pain were becoming more frequent and more debilitating. It was time to get rid of them.

That February, on Chris's birthday, we talked about getting a new dog. Chris had been sleeping upstairs on the sofa because the hallucinations were so bad when he went downstairs. I told him that I would get him a new puppy for his birthday, but he had to be able to sleep downstairs to take care of it.

Chris missed Hazzard terribly and was really excited about a puppy. I suggested a smaller dog this time. To tell the truth, the idea came from some commercial that showed dogs and their owners looking alike. With his sad expression and long, blond lashes, Chris reminded me of a cocker spaniel.

I started taking Chris to pet stores and we'd look at the puppies; with every shopping trip, Chris got more and more excited about getting a dog. He started talking about it constantly, and even began to dream about his new puppy. That was when I knew that it was working: his subconscious was on board.

Sure enough, the figures of Chris's abuse started meeting gruesome deaths. One melted in front of Chris like plastic left near a stove, until it was just an ectoplasmic puddle bubbling on the floor. Jacques started to fall apart, literally — his body parts would fall off and drop on the floor, and he would have to pick them up and reattach them. Chris's subconscious had a poetic sensibility: Jacques's penis fell off the most frequently. Finally, he started becoming unable to reassemble himself, and he started showing up with pieces missing. In the end, he collapsed into a pile of blobby flesh and vanished.

We found a pet store that had puppies for sale at a reasonable price. They even had cocker spaniel pups, but that batch was spoken for. Chris got to hold one, though, a little blonde girl that licked his hand, then curled up on his chest and fell asleep. He had such a hard time giving her back, my heart hurt for him. The store owner promised to call us when the next batch of spaniels came in.

That night, Chris was watching television while I cleared the dining room table. Suddenly, he shot up in his seat and yelled, "*FUCK, yeah!*" I couldn't see why he was so excited; there was a comedy on, and it was good, but not *that* good.

"Ursula just disappeared! She was standing in the doorway to the basement, looking sad. She'd been looking for Jacques ever since he disappeared last week. Anyway, I saw her watching me from the doorway, and I just thought, 'Fuck you, you're going to die just like Jacques did, how do you like that, you bitch?' And she just melted down and disappeared. She's fucking *gone!*"

A week later, the pet store owner called. We went down to look at the new puppies. They weren't exactly cocker spaniels: they were smaller and their coats were curly. But they had the longish ears and spaniel-like faces.

Chris picked up another little girl. She was pale blonde with chocolate eyes, and so small that she fit in one of his hands. She looked like an adorable little stuffed toy.

"They are not pure cocker spaniel. There's some poodle, so they don't shed. You cut the hair when it gets long."

I pulled a poker face and tried to remember how Frank bargained people down. "Well, we were looking for a cocker spaniel. I was kind of expecting that when you called, you would have one for us."

Chris held the puppy against his chest as if he were afraid that I would snatch it away from him. "Mom, I don't mind, really. I'd be happy with one of these puppies." So much for bargaining.

The store owner kept going: "I could take a hundred dollars off the price if you wanted to take it today." I was tempted, but Chris still had one hallucination hanging around, so he still couldn't sleep downstairs.

Chris knew what I was thinking. "Mom, if we buy one now, I'll sleep downstairs tonight. I don't care. I really want to get a puppy today. This one is perfect. I'm going to name her Daisy, after Daisy Duke."

Well, once you name it, I guess you better buy it. "Okay, we'll take this one."

When we climbed in the car, Chris suddenly looked out the window. "The last hallucination just evaporated! I saw him! Mom, they're all gone! I don't see any of them anymore." The whole ride home, he held his new baby on his lap and gazed out the window with a look of utter peacefulness.

That night, Chris was downstairs in his apartment for the first time in a year. He didn't sleep much, though, because he was up watching Daisy all night long.

Chapter Thirty-Six

"Medicine!!!"

I was learning a bit about heavy metal music by now. Chris had never heard of The Beatles or The Who, but he could tell you the names of every member of every speed metal band in existence. And their brands of guitar. And the lyrics to most of their songs. And the year each album was released. And nearly anything else you could want to know about them.

The band Metallica was making a comeback after three years out of the studio, and they were being honoured by MuchMusic with an episode of *Icon*. At one point, several fans were brought up to the stage to give one-word descriptions of the band. Most of them were predictably laudatory, but one man — a pretty hardcore metalhead by the look of him — gave the heavy metal salute and roared out, "*Medicine!!!*" I couldn't understand his comment, but Chris knew exactly what he was talking about.

The lyrics to these songs (which I had to read from the album notes, because I couldn't make out what they were singing) were actually powerful expressions of angry feelings, loss and betrayal, bitterness, and hatred of the world. They were a way to give an honest voice to the feelings that most songs avoided — that, in fact, most people avoided. These were the feelings that abuse victims need to access and express, and when I watched Chris headbanging in the basement with his earphones on and his face screwed up in concentration, I understood what the hardcore metalhead had meant by "medicine."

When Metallica's album *St. Anger* came out, Chris got the CD, and the DVD of the recording sessions. We watched it together about a dozen times, and it was a perfect description of Chris's feelings about anger. It made me wonder exactly where James Hetfield had been coming from when he wrote the songs. Even the cover art, a monstrous angel bound and in agony, was symbolic of the outrage in Chris's mind.

Chris's dreams became more specific — he was invited to be a member of Metallica, and he was friends with all the other members. He became obsessed with the band, reading magazines and books on them, watching their DVDs over and over, and headbanging for hours to their music. This fascination with Metallica seemed to block out a lot of his negative symptoms — there were fewer nightmares and less hallucinating as he focused on the band.

He also began to get angrier during our evening talks, ranting about his family in particular. His earlier anger had seemed confused, constricted by self-doubt and fear; it felt the way the "St. Anger" angel looked. His outrage during this period seemed to bleed out strong and clean, expressed with more confidence that he had been treated wrongly. He had found another source of informal therapy.

When I found out that Metallica was coming to Toronto, I got tickets. Chris was ecstatic, but the six-month wait was going to be a problem. He obsessed about going, and worried about something going wrong to make him miss the concert.

I decided to try to find other concerts for him to attend in the meantime. Toronto has a huge variety of music venues, and I checked the local free press for metal bands.

Our first concert was an appearance by Iron Maiden at the Air Canada Centre. Chris was elated. I went with him, since I wasn't sure how he would handle the crowd or finding his way around the massive venue — Chris frequently got lost when I took him to Walmart. And I was pretty excited myself — I hadn't been to a concert in over twenty years. The place was sold out, and the crowd was gigantic but well behaved.

Chris was weirdly quiet while we looked for our seats, and I had a feeling that he was dissociating already. I suggested that he get a T-shirt, and he agreed without much emotion. I had to help him choose the one he wanted, and he had a hard time asking the vendor for it — I finally went over and helped him with it. We found our seats, which were great, and all the people around us were really excited, but Chris still looked like a zombie. I was starting to get worried.

The concert was amazing — Bruce Dickinson worked the crowd like a maestro, and the stage effects really sold the music. I didn't even know Iron Maiden, and I loved it. But Chris sat numbly throughout the whole thing.

I was a bit perturbed by the end of the evening. After we got to the car, I asked him, "Didn't you like the concert?"

"Yeah, it was great."

"You sure didn't look like you were enjoying it."

"I was just amazed by the whole thing. I was just sitting there the whole time, thinking, 'Holy shit, I'm actually seeing Iron Maiden live!' This was the best night of my life! Thanks for taking me."

That night, Chris dreamed of being in Iron Maiden instead of Metallica, but the dreams were still very positive.

He was hyper about the experience for a few days, and he wore the shirt everywhere.

So we started buying tickets for local heavy metal bands. The venues were smaller, and I didn't think it was cool for Chris to be going with his mom, so he started going by himself. The first time he went solo, he told me afterward: "I almost went back to the car. Then I told myself, 'You've gotta try it. Nobody's going to kill you in there.' So I walked up and stood in line. I even started talking to the people next to me. There was this young couple, and we hung out during the concert. I bought a few beers, but the guy drank a bit too much and I had to take him to the bathroom to throw up. They took my cell number, and they're gonna call me and maybe hang out." He was let down for a few days that the new friends never phoned, but the idea that he could go out on his own was really exciting to both of us.

It startled me that Chris could be so confident when I wasn't around, talking to strangers and ordering beers, and yet so meek and withdrawn when I was there.

I started to learn a bit more about the heavy metal bands that Chris listened to, and it didn't surprise me that most of them had members who had come from troubled families; some even had histories of physical or sexual abuse. I wondered if this was why the music resonated with Chris in such a deep way: the voice of anger in the music was giving his own anger a voice.

After six months, Chris went to the Metallica concert. Wouldn't you know it, Frank had a medical emergency going on, and I couldn't take him. Bobby and his brother took the extra tickets and were happy to bring Chris to the concert, so he got there after all. He had a fantastic time — the only problem was when the pyrotechnics frightened

Bobby, who was terrified of loud noises, but Chris helped to talk him down.

Overall, I think that Chris went to about forty concerts that year, including Mötley Crüe, Guns N' Roses, Cannibal Corpse, and Korn. They became another therapy tool for him. He even crowd-surfed once, and went into the mosh pit a few times. His most memorable time was at a Megadeth concert where he was standing right by the stage, singing along with Dave Mustaine through every song. Dave apparently noticed that Chris knew all the songs, and gave him a grin.

After about half a year, Chris got interested in another band, Slipknot. The group has probably the most heavy metal sound you can imagine — if a psychotic episode had a soundtrack, this would be it. They also have an unusual stage presence: nine musicians in horror masks and jumpsuits. Chris became fascinated by this group. He would watch their videos and headbang to their music for hours. He knew all the members by name, and had dreams of joining the band.

I couldn't really deal with Slipknot — the artwork is gory, and the lyrics to their songs are bitter and deliberately ugly. But this music resonated with Chris in a particular way. It gave me some insight into Chris; I wondered if I could ever understand just how deep the damage was from the years of abuse.

So when Slipknot came to Toronto, I got a ticket for him. Chris was ecstatic. When I picked him up, he was proudly wearing a T-shirt with a picture of an eviscerated body on the front. "I was right up front, where the mosh pit was. I even crowd-surfed!" The concerts made Chris feel like he was part of something — like he belonged.

Chapter Thirty-Seven

Melting the Iceberg

A new symptom showed up around this time: hysterical blindness.

We were watching television one evening when I noticed that Chris wasn't looking at the TV. I asked if he was getting a new memory.

"Uhh, no. Don't panic, Mom, but I can't see right now. It'll go away in a few minutes." He seemed very calm about it, so I tried not to overreact. I guess it was a measure of how weird our lives had become that we just kept on watching — or listening to — our show while the episode of blindness took its course.

Chris remembered having this symptom before, back in high school. "It was when the stuff was still happening with Ursula and Jacques. I would be in class and all of a sudden I couldn't see anything for a few minutes. Or things would go black and white. I figured it was the drugs, I was smoking up a lot back then. Ursula took me to get my eyes checked but there wasn't anything wrong with them. It stopped by itself after a while."

I'd heard of hysterical blindness before, but I'd never actually seen it happening. Chris would start to see the world in shades of grey, as if he were watching a black-and-white television screen. Then everything would go completely black for a few minutes. Sometimes he would see me against a black background, and other times he would see nothing but darkness. I noticed that he didn't walk into furniture or miss doorways during these episodes; it was as if part of his brain was still "seeing" even if his conscious mind wasn't.

As if this weren't enough to deal with, Chris was showing signs of crisis. He was throwing up more often, he was very irritable, and zombies were starting to show up in his nightmares.

Strangely, Chris began to have hallucinations about zombies as well. His previous hallucinations (or, strictly speaking, dissociative episodes) were excruciatingly realistic: he saw his abusers in detail, down to their freckles and beard stubble. These new hallucinations were equally detailed, but they were characters from his nightmares. It was as if the barrier between his conscious and subconscious minds had become permeable and the grotesque creatures of his imagination were leaking out to inhabit his daytime world.

In a new series of nightmares, Chris was in the kitchen of Jacques's house; a zombie was sitting at the kitchen table, talking to him, waiting for the other members of its club to arrive. It was as if a Saturday night card game for zombies was scheduled.

While we were discussing this dream during one of our nightly sessions, Chris got a memory breakthrough about other abusers. "I remember this guy Louis, he was a friend of Jacques's, and Ursula would drop me off at his house some evenings. They had a schedule for who was going to get me on which night. Jacques had a calendar on his fridge, I remember seeing it in the kitchen at his house. One time, Ursula was complaining, 'I want to do things to him tonight,' and Jacques was telling her, 'Now, baby, it's Louis's turn tonight, we get him this weekend.'

"Ursula would tell everybody at home that I was going to spend the weekend at a friend's house. I would have to pack a bag and everything. I remember I would throw up before getting in the car with her. (I think that's why I always have to throw up before I go in the car with you, Mom — I just realized that.)

"Louis was really skinny, and he had sores around his nose all the time. He used to snort coke and he would try to get me to try it. He wasn't into hurting me the way Jacques and the others were, but he used to watch me go to the bathroom. He said I didn't like having sex with guys because nobody had done it to me the right way yet.

"One time, Louis had me handcuffed and shackled. He left his gun on the hall table when he went to the bathroom. I picked it up. I was thinking of shooting him but I was afraid of going to jail. So when he came out, I was waiting by the door; I hit him in the back of the head with the gun butt and knocked him out. I got the handcuff keys out of his pants pocket, and I was dressed and out of there before he woke up. I walked all the way back to my house."

After that recovered memory, I waited to see if Chris's symptoms would subside. Instead, the hysterical blindness started to get worse, and he started to get short periods of deafness. He could usually hear my voice, but he couldn't listen to his music or the television. It started happening when we were out shopping or walking the dogs in the park; Chris hated that most of all, since he didn't like acting strange in public. He would tell me when an episode was starting; I would hold his hand and keep talking to him, and we would just stand around casually until it was over.

We were still going to the cottage on weekends and bringing Connor up with us. He had a new little brother at home and my daughter-in-law needed the break, so we took him pretty often that summer. Connor was into camping now, since he had gone on a camping trip with his parents the previous year. Chris was willing to take him, so I bought a tent and some camping bags. We set the tent up about thirty feet away from the cottage, so I could keep an eye on things, but it still counted as camping to Connor. He and Chris were out there all night, with chips and Coke and their flashlights.

This experience triggered a memory for Chris: "Jacques used to take me camping. It would be him and Ursula, and Jim and Dave. They would bring tents and camping gear and spend the weekend out in the woods, with no other people around.

"I really hated those camping trips. They would sleep in the tents, and they made me sleep outside on the ground. I remember them sitting around the campfire roasting hot dogs, and if I got too close they would throw burning sticks at me. I would wait until they all fell asleep, and then sneak into the food tent and eat potato chips.

"One night, Jim made me stand at attention for hours. He told me, 'If you move a muscle, I'll kill you. I've got a thermos of coffee, and we're going to be up all night.' It was weird; he talked about his army experiences the whole time like we were old buddies, but he would hit me if I even blinked — then he'd keep talking like nothing had happened.

"Another time, they stuck me in a sleeping bag and tied the open end with a rope; then they hung the sleeping bag up on a tree branch and used me as a piñata. They would hit the sleeping bag with sticks, but it didn't hurt too much because the bag was some protection. But it was really hot inside there, and I was afraid I would suffocate. I nearly passed out, but I was able to reach the zipper at the bottom of the bag and open it. I fell out on the ground, and they all laughed."

Chris looked thoughtful. "I think that the worst part of it was that they were all doing normal camping things and enjoying it — and at the same time they enjoyed it even more because they got to treat me like a thing or an animal. I started to feel like that's what I was, that I wasn't even human anymore. It was just less confusing to go along with it and think of myself that way."

Chris and I had often talked about whether we should try to turn in his abusers. I was worried that they would still be molesting other boys. Chris seemed somehow sure that they weren't, but couldn't explain why he felt that way. I thought that it was wishful thinking on his part. I knew that he was afraid of going to the police. This seems to be an almost universal characteristic of abuse victims: the fear of disclosing the abuse. When I asked Chris about this, he looked at me as if I were simple-minded. "They won't believe me, Mom. It's my word against Ursula's. I tried telling people before. I even told a cop once. He brought me over to Jacques's house, and Jacques told him that I was his nephew and I was mentally disturbed. The cop believed him and left me with Jacques. I remember watching the cop walking up the driveway back to his patrol car and thinking, 'Wait ... come back and listen to me ... well, fuck you too!' Jacques was an ex-cop — who was going to believe me over him? And Ursula could go to the school or the doctors and tell them anything she wanted, and nobody ever questioned her."

A few evenings after that conversation, during our nightly talk, Chris recovered a memory of the deaths of Jim and Dave.

"These guys were long-haul truckers, and they used drugs to stay awake, besides the drugs I saw them taking during the abuse sessions. They died in a head-on collision with a car. I remember seeing it on the news. It was a small red car, I didn't know what make it was, but it was totalled. There was a family of five in the car, I think they were black, their pictures were on the television, they all died too. I felt bad for them, but I was so glad that Jim and Dave were dead.

"After the accident, Jacques was different. He drank a lot, almost as much as my dad, and he started using drugs more. He really started going downhill, I remember that he got a really big beer gut. He and Ursula broke up, they stopped having sex together even though they would still rape me. I think Ursula was a little scared of Jacques by then."

Chris was recovering memories from a whole other period of abuse, after we had thought that this part of his illness was over. It felt like a huge setback, although my readings had taught me that memories can happen in separate waves. It felt like going back to square one.

Almost three years after moving in with us, Chris did appear to be at the same point in his illness, and this frustrated him. He still rarely left the house without me, and couldn't be left home alone for long. He still needed hours per day of talking out his anxieties. His compulsive behaviours, like flicking light switches on and off when he left a room, were just as frequent. He still had a terrible time concentrating and remembering even simple things, and depended on his daily routine to keep him focused.

I remember seeing a photo of an iceberg once; it showed both the mountain above the waterline and the enormous asteroid of ice beneath the water. It made a good metaphor for Chris's illness — on the surface, there was always the same amount of dysfunction visible. As one area cleared off, more problems came up. But underneath, the overall mass of damage was getting smaller. And there was a difference in Chris himself, a new confidence that showed through the damage. I doubt that a psychiatrist would have considered him healthier — but I could see that he was taking things more in stride. He was holding onto the activities he enjoyed, music and video games in particular, to ground him when the memories got bad. And he had resources that weren't there before.

CHAPTER THIRTY-EIGHT

THE FAMILY THAT PREYS TOGETHER...

There was one thing in Chris's life that he was extremely happy about — his father's family was no longer involved with him. We hadn't heard from them in over a year, and my old agency hadn't been in contact with us either. I had almost forgotten about them, and even Chris was starting to think of them in the past tense. He still missed his uncle and his younger cousin George, but he was relieved beyond words that his father and aunt were out of his life. It never occurred to me that they might still be focused on him after all this time.

By sheer chance, Chris ran across his cousin at a coffee shop near our house. George was happy to see him, and they talked for awhile. George was still living with his family, and couldn't wait to move out. "His parents argued a lot. I remembered one morning when my uncle said he was leaving, and my aunt said, 'It's about time. Nobody's going to miss you!' And my uncle said, 'I meant I'm going to work!' Other than arguing, they barely talked. It was pretty tense at the house."

George told Chris about a family meeting that had happened a few weeks earlier. Even Chris's sister and grandfather had been there. The topic had been what to do about Chris leaving the family, and apparently feelings had run pretty high.

"George said that everybody was really mad at me for moving in with you and not talking to any of them anymore. My uncle told them, 'Why not just leave him alone? He's not hurting anybody.' They just jumped all over him like he'd said the worst thing in the world.

"Even George thought it was weird how upset they were. My grandfather called me a traitor to the family, and even my own sister was badmouthing me. I can't believe that they're still freaking out like this after all this time.

"The strangest thing is, George said everybody was talking about how to get me back into the family again, like it was really important. I don't understand. It's not like they worried about me when I was living with Dan and Denise, or Barbara. Nobody even seemed upset when I tried to kill myself."

I remembered back to my university days, and a psychology course I had taken. Back then, a psychotherapist named Virginia Satir had developed a theory of family systems. I had learned about scapegoating — some families pick one family member that is the "bad one," that they can blame for anything that goes wrong. As long as they have that person, they don't have to deal with problems in the family itself. But if they lose that person then the whole system breaks down and the family sort of falls apart. But this reaction still seemed pretty extreme at this point.

"I guess they're worried about what you're telling me," I told Chris. "You're carrying a lot of family secrets. Even if they say they don't believe you, they don't want anyone else believing you. And they know that I do. But they don't have any power over your life anymore. You haven't anything to worry about."

And that's when Eddie started stalking Chris again.

A week or so after the conversation with George, Chris walked over to the Internet café one evening for a beer and there was his father using one of the computers. The last we had heard, Eddie was living in a different part of the city, so Chris was surprised to see him only a block away from our house. Chris tried to avoid his father and finished his beer as fast as he could, but Eddie came over and started trying to chat with him. Since they were in a public place, Chris maintained his temper but still managed to give Eddie an earful. Then he came straight home to tell me about it.

"I couldn't believe it. I haven't seen my ex-father in two years, I guess, and he manages to show up just when I'm at the café. He was on the computer when I got there, but it was like he was watching for me: he saw me right away. He looked really old. His teeth were disgusting, and his clothes were messy. It was kind of creepy — he looked like a homeless person. Just like a bum on the street.

"So he came up to me and started telling me how much I was disappointing the family, and how I owe it to them to stay in touch. He told me that he had an email address now and tried to give it to me so I could write to him. I told him that I didn't want to stay in touch with him or my ex-relatives. He had Janice's email address too, but I told him I didn't want that either. I said that he and the family just wanted me back so they could control me, and that wasn't going to happen anymore, not ever. They didn't want to hear about the stuff that happened to me? Well, they didn't have to. They just had to leave me the hell alone. Anyway, I was getting pretty loud and people were starting to look at us, so I told him to fuck off and I left."

Chris was pretty stressed out by the incident, but he was also remarkably elated by having been able to yell at Eddie. It was such a profound change from him being afraid of upsetting his father or aunt only two years earlier. I felt very proud of him.

I also felt a little troubled by the timing of this episode. Just after the family meeting that George had warned us about, Eddie shows up — with an email address for Chris to contact. The whole thing seemed suspicious.

A week later, Chris ran into his father again. He was taking a walk around the block, and Eddie was parked just a few doors down from our house. He rolled his window down and called Chris over.

"It was gross. Eddie was crying and telling me that he knew he had treated me badly, but he wanted to make it up to me. I told him that there was no way he could do that, I hated his guts and the only thing I wished was that he was back to my age so I could beat the shit out of him.

"Then Eddie stuck his arm out of the window and told me to hit him, just go ahead and hit him. I kind of punched him on the arm, real light, but it just felt stupid. It was frustrating, I wanted to beat him up the way he did to me when I was a kid, but now I'm a grown man and he's just an old, sick, pathetic fuck. I just wouldn't have felt right about it. But it's crazy, feeling so mad and not being able to do anything about it.

"But I could feel myself getting angry, my face felt really hot, and I yelled at him to get the fuck out of here and never come back or I would beat him to death and enjoy doing it. He looked really scared, and he started the car and took off. I looked around, and there were people across the street kind of staring at me, it was kind of embarrassing, so I just came home."

This confirmed my suspicions: Chris's family was trying to re-establish contact with him, and using Eddie to do it. I couldn't think of anything to do about this, other than ride it out and hope they'd get tired of it. In the meantime, it was rather therapeutic for Chris to be able to let out his anger at his father, even if it meant making a spectacle of himself occasionally.

I was interested in Chris's conundrum, being angry at his father but unable to fight him. This must happen to other abuse victims — by the time they are adults and able to deal with their past, they must come to grips with the present state of their abusers. I wonder if this is another reason why so few victims prosecute: life beats them to the punch by aging their tormentors into weak, pathetic shadows of their former selves. I could see how frustrated Chris was — enraged at the violent giant of his childhood and finally ready to fight back against him, only to find that the giant no longer existed.

Old or not, Eddie had plenty of mischief left in him. He began stalking Chris on a regular basis, frequently showing up at the Internet café and other places too. One of the few places Chris would go on his own was the nearby dog park. The dogs loved being able to run free, and Chris had an opportunity to chat with the other owners. He felt very comfortable there; it was one of his few safe places.

That is, until Eddie happened to run into Chris on his way home from the park.

"It was getting dark, and I was bringing the dogs home. I was about a block from the house, across from the Tim Hortons, when I saw Eddie on the sidewalk up ahead, coming toward us. When he got close, Daisy started barking and Nika growled at him, so he kind of kept his distance. I stopped under a streetlight and asked him what he was doing there.

"He started in with the same old shit, how I'm hurting the family by not talking to anyone, how I'm a bad son. I told him the same things as I did before, but he didn't stop. He was slurring his words, I don't know if he was drunk or not, but he didn't make a lot of sense. Anyway, I told him off for about five minutes, then I walked away and brought the dogs home."

Eddie started becoming a regular on Chris's trips home from the dog park. I got Chris to vary his schedule, but Eddie would still show up. I couldn't figure out how he was doing it — he would have to be staking out the street for hours just to harass Chris for ten minutes.

And I could see that it was starting to wear Chris down. Instead of being relaxed from his walks, he would come home stressed out from his encounters with Eddie. I would have to talk him down for hours after every outing. It was opening old wounds, bringing back memories of his childhood as well as his time living at Olga's house and having to please everybody all the time.

The problem was, there was no way to stop Eddie from talking to Chris on a public street. The only way to stop him was for Chris to give up walking the dogs, which was a big part of his day. And even if he did, Eddie could show up at any other time that Chris tried to go out by himself. The only ways to avoid Eddie were to go out with me in the car or stay in the house. It infuriated me that these damned people could still come up with a way to control Chris's life.

CHAPTER THIRTY-NINE

IT SMELLS LIKE ... VICTORY!

One option that occurred to me was a restraining order. I had never tried to get one before, and it seemed a bit like overkill. I wasn't even sure that this situation would warrant a restraining order, at least to other people. It was something that abused wives got as protection against their spouses. How could we justify it to stop an old man from talking to his son?

As the weeks went on and Eddie showed no sign of stopping, the idea of a restraining order began to make more sense. I phoned the Peel Regional Police and they mailed me a form. It didn't look like much work — if this was all it took, we had nothing to lose by trying.

I let Chris fill in the form, even though his handwriting looks like a third-grader's; I felt that he needed to get out some of his frustrations at Eddie by doing the paperwork himself. I hedged our bet, however, with a write-up of my own explaining the whole situation between them, from the childhood abuse, to the sexual abuse, which Eddie was too drunk to stop, to the abandonment of Chris in his teens. I hoped that this would make our request seem more reasonable to a judge.

We took the application form to the courthouse, an imposing building whose austere architecture added to its intimidation factor. The first thing we encountered was the line for the metal detector at the building entrance. It was just like the one at the airport, only with more uniformed guards. We were then sent to a long waiting room where we were eventually given a number and sent to another waiting room. Finally, a worker helped us process the restraining order request. The worker explained that the next step was going to be an appointment with a mediator at the courthouse; the date was over a month away, which was frustrating. We also had to officially serve Eddie with a notice of the mediation meeting, explaining that Chris was seeking the restraining order against him. Since we didn't have an address for Eddie, I used the home address for his sister, Olga.

The idea of the mediation meeting unnerved Chris, reawakening his old fears that people wouldn't believe him. On the way home, he erupted in an anxiety attack. "Mom, it's my word against Eddie's. And what if my ex-aunt and my ex-grandfather show up and tell them that I'm a liar and that I'm the one causing problems for the family? They've been doing this to me all my life, and they could do it again."

"Chris, you aren't doing it alone this time. I'll be there with you. And I'm not sure that Eddie can bring people with him, at least not his whole family. If you can face him on the street, you can face him in a courtroom."

I wasn't as confident as I sounded. I kept picturing the restraining-order paperwork arriving at Olga's house, complete with my write-up about what a rotten father Eddie had been, and, worst of all, mentioning the sexual abuse, which the family still refused to acknowledge. This was all about to go public for the first time. I could imagine Olga's head exploding when she read it. Chris was right about one thing: his ex-family was probably not going to take this lying down.

But the next month passed without incident, other than the ongoing harassment by Eddie. I sometimes wondered if Chris actually got something out of these confrontations. There was a lifetime of anger for him to let out, and this was finally an opportunity to do it. Chris was certainly willing to keep walking the dogs every evening, even when I suggested going out earlier to try avoiding Eddie. He came home from the encounters genuinely upset, but there was an excitement in the way he described striking back at Eddie verbally, even intimidating this monster of his childhood. I guess you take your therapy anyway you can find it.

Finally, the morning came for the mediation meeting. Chris wore a suit and tie, and I power-dressed in one of my social worker outfits. I reminded Chris that this was just a part of the process, not the final judgment for the restraining order. Still, we were both pretty nervous as we passed through the metal detectors and checked in at the waiting room. Finally, we were called to the mediation room, which was as large as a courtroom but less formal. We were the only ones there besides the mediator, sitting behind a long table. Every sound we made walking to our chairs echoed in the empty room, adding self-consciousness to the nerve cocktail stirring around in our heads.

And there was Eddie. He was sitting in the bank of chairs on the other side of the room at one of the smaller tables, facing the mediator. He didn't look over as we sat down at the other table. Chris was rigid; I couldn't tell if it was from fear or anger, but it wasn't a good sign.

The mediator had a copy of our application — we had brought our own from home — and began by asking fairly simple questions to confirm the information on the form. Chris had to answer some of the questions, but I helped out as much as I could. Actually, Chris was focusing pretty well, which made me think of how he would have handled this situation three years earlier. I was so proud of him.

Then the mediator began to ask questions of Eddie, and my feelings turned to total shock. This man who had been the terror of Chris's life was a blithering idiot. He couldn't even remember his own address. This wasn't the man I had met three years earlier. He sounded either drunk or senile. I turned to really look at him, and Chris had been right: Eddie looked like a homeless person. His clothes didn't fit him anymore, his hair was whitened and had barely been combed, and there was a scruff of whiskers on his jowls. He kept his head down and his eyes on the table, never looking at us once. I hated the idea of feeling sorry for this man, but I couldn't help it — he was pathetic.

I turned my focus back to the mediator, who was wrapping up the session. She recommended that the process continue to the next stage, which would be a hearing before a judge. The court date was several weeks away, since there wasn't a question of danger to Chris. The mediator mentioned that restraining orders were usually issued for spouse-abuse situations, and suggested that a peace bond might be an alternative to explore.

Chris handled Eddie's presence at the hearing with remarkable restraint. On the way home, however, he was upset by the experience. "I had a feeling that they weren't going to take this lying down. I knew he was going to show up. The family probably made him do it."

"I'm inclined to agree with you about that. I don't think that Eddie could have found his way up here on his own, or even remembered the date and time for the session by himself. Olga or your grandfather probably made him come.

"By the way, you were right about Eddie going downhill. I hardly recognized him. He sure doesn't look like anyone to be scared of anymore."

"I'm not scared of the sonofabitch. I just hate his guts, I want him to leave me alone. The only time I want to hear about him is when he's dead, and then I'm gonna go piss on his grave."

"It must be weird, though, when someone who's been abusing you all your life turns old and weak like that. In a way, it must be kind of satisfying, like getting even."

"Not really. I mean, I can yell at him when I see him, but what I really want to do is beat the shit out of him, and I can't because he's an old man and can't fight back. I fantasize about him being thirty years younger and me being my age now. I'd kill his ass. But now all I can do is yell at him.

"And it's not like he's owning up to what he did to me, either. He keeps making excuses or blaming me for everything, or telling me I have to forgive him because he's old and sick. It's hard to explain, but it still feels like he's abusing me and kind of getting off on it. He's showing me that I can't get away from him."

But it was amazing that Eddie had deteriorated so much, as if he had aged ten years in the past three. I thought back to the account of Olga's family meeting, and their obsession with Chris's "defection." Could the loss of his own victim/scapegoat have affected Eddie to this extent? Surely there were other factors, such as age and alcoholism, but they had been there before. It would be interesting to find out if other abusers had the same reaction.

But the meeting had left us with something else to think about. The mediator had said that the restraining order might not be appropriate for Chris's circumstances. I knew something about peace bonds, and I was pretty sure we would have to bring charges against Eddie in order to get one. And Chris was nowhere near ready to charge anyone yet. He wouldn't be able to handle the process, and he was far too sick to be a credible witness. I could imagine the damage it would cause him if Eddie wasn't convicted, or if the charges were dismissed.

So it was a restraining order — or nothing. The weeks passed reasonably well. Eddie cut down on his evening dialogues with Chris — I had been hoping that he would be intimidated by the legal proceedings — and Chris seemed more confident since the mediation meeting, looking forward to having some control over the situation at last. But I was worried that Chris's situation wouldn't warrant a restraining order. And I wasn't sure how it would affect Chris if his plea for help were rejected. It had happened so many times in his life already.

Finally, the day of the hearing arrived. We went to the courthouse in the morning, even though the hearing was in the afternoon, because we had to see a lawyer for a consultation first. The process was the same — the metal detectors, the wait to get the appointment, and finally a nervous hour's wait outside the lawyer's office door until he arrived to speak with us.

Our lawyer seemed remarkably casual as he perused our application paperwork. Then he calmly told us, "This judge only gives restraining orders for marital cases, such as spousal abuse. I've never heard of her giving one for anything else, so I don't want you to get your hopes up."

"Don't you come to the court as well? I thought you were going to represent us, you know, to be our lawyer."

"No, Chris will represent himself. The judge might ask him a few questions, but usually it's nothing very complicated.

I'm just here to make sure the paperwork's in order, and it is. I can see you've got a real situation here, and I wish you luck."

The hearing wasn't until that afternoon, so Chris and I went to a nearby coffee shop for a very tense lunch. I found it hard to eat, and Chris went to the bathroom and vomited even worse than usual. It was frustrating to be taken through these weeks of hope and worrying, just to be told that Chris's situation wasn't serious enough for a restraining order. We didn't talk much as we went back to the courthouse.

This time, we were finally in the courtroom itself. It looked like the stage set from *Judge Judy*, but it felt very real and kind of intimidating. The judge was a pleasant-looking woman in her early forties, much kinder looking than Judge Judy, and I was grateful for that at least. I wasn't sure how Chris would handle being cross-examined when his case came up. We both knew that he would have to present the case by himself.

There were several cases before ours, so we sat in the gallery area and waited. Then the weirdest thing happened. It was as if the old Gypsy Curse was having a last kick at us. We had been told to turn off our cellphones in the courtroom, and I was sure — absolutely sure — that mine was off. I saw Chris turn his off. Then, about ten minutes into the court session, Chris's phone rang. He has a particularly loud ring tone, and it seemed to echo in the courtroom. I felt that everyone was looking at us. Chris grabbed the phone by the second ring and answered it, but there was nobody there. The guard, a big burly black guy in a police uniform, gave us a dirty look. I checked Chris's phone myself to make sure it was off.

Five minutes later, Chris's phone rings again; again, there was no one there. This time, the guard came over and politely warned us that phones needed to be turned off. I pulled the battery out of Chris's phone to make sure it wouldn't happen again.

A few minutes later, *my* phone rings — a quieter tone, but still very noticeable in the silence. Now everyone was looking at us. I got up and left the courtroom to see who was calling, as I figured it must be Frank trying to reach us for something important. Again, there was nobody there. The guard poked his head out to remind me again that cellphone use was not allowed in the courtroom. I pulled my battery out and showed it to him. "I'd like to see it ring now!" I said. He grinned and held the door open for me.

Just then, Chris's case was called. I watched him walk firmly to the table in front of the judge's desk and take his seat. It was nerve-wracking not being able to help him, but we both knew this was something he would have to do on his own. He sat calmly with his hands folded on the table in front of him while the judge read the form. When she got to the addendum I had added, I could see her eyes widen as she read on.

Then the judge began to question Chris about his relationship with his father. I wasn't even listening to her, I was so intent on Chris. Suddenly I was seeing a young man of twenty-four years, in his new suit bought just for the occasion, self-confident and mature, responding in a firm voice to the excruciating queries being put to him.

This was the person Chris had been meant to be all along, the person his abusers had tried and failed to destroy. It was a revelation to me, so used to seeing him frightened, or sick, or confused. In that moment, the promise of Chris — a whole, healthy, independent Chris — was a tangible reality.

Finally, the judge was ready with her decision. I found myself actually holding my breath as she spoke. "As you may have been told, the restraining order is used most frequently in marital or long-term relationships where one partner requires recourse against harassment from the other. I do not usually order it in other situations." My heart literally sank into my stomach.

But then she pursed her lips as she lifted the form in front of her. "However, this situation is unusual, and I believe that protection would be appropriate in this case. I am therefore prepared to issue the requested restraining order." She stamped a rubber seal on the paper and handed it to the woman sitting next to her.

Chris thanked her and returned to me on the bench. I totally blew his newfound air of dignity by squashing him in a bear hug, but he didn't seem to mind: he was grinning from ear to ear. We both knew that we had won more than the right to tell Eddie to piss off.

For the first time in his life, Chris had been given power over an abuser.

For the first time in his life, the system had listened and believed and been on his side.

For the first time in his life, his story had been respected, his experiences had mattered.

And he had done it himself.

As we left the court that afternoon carrying the restraining order as if it were the Holy Grail, I knew that it was not going to magically solve all our problems or make Chris well any faster. There were still nightmares and flashbacks and memories to look forward to, maybe for years to come. Weighed against all the struggles yet to come, all the years of terrible damage to deal with, maybe this would seem insignificant. And yet...

I smiled as I sniffed the Xerox odour of the stiff pages. It smelled like victory.

Epilogue

As you may have guessed, our victory in court is hardly the end of the story. Actually, Chris and I have been working on his healing for the past sixteen years, and the events of this book were just the start of the journey. When I started writing, I began to realize around the four-hundredth page of the manuscript that I was going to have to break up the story into two or three volumes, or it would end up longer than *Moby-Dick* — and just as exhausting. Reading on a topic like child sexual abuse is like eating an elephant: it is best done one bite at a time.

My editors have been bugging me for more on Chris's mother's family, and his childhood in North Bay. That was actually something we had checked out soon after the hearing, when Chris and his father's family pretty much wrote each other off. Chris still had Christmas and summer visits with his maternal aunts and their families, and we even made a couple of trips up north to visit his childhood home. In some ways, it was therapeutic — he did connect more with his childhood. However, in the end, it also answered the question of why Chris never asked them for help.

Chris also began developing friendships around this time, and we learned that, for people with PTSD, relationships come with unique difficulties. One of the friends he made was an ex-soldier with PTSD from his time in the military. I learned that these types of trauma disorders can be very different.

The biggest takeaway we learned was that there was a dearth of resources for men with PTSD, or for anyone with Chris's level of trauma. That situation still persists. One of our biggest miracles was finding Dr. Michael Irving, a Toronto therapist and artist whose sculpture is on the cover of *Lazarus Heart*. You can read more about his project in the appendix, and more about him in the next book.

I would like to leave you with a little gift: a poem I wrote about Chris's struggle. So many times he has wanted to give up, and I could understand: PTSD can be a living hell. But I would remind him that survival was his biggest victory — first, surviving the abuse itself, and then surviving the healing process. If he could do one, he had to be strong enough to be able to do the other. And every day was a part of that victory.

EVERY DAY YOU STAY ALIVE

Is one more victory you score
    In the war
    For something more
A battle fought heart beat by beat
For solid ground beneath your feet

Is clean, relentless, healing pain
    As poisons drain
    And old scars strain
Against the healthy tissue grown
From broken brain and broken bone

Is defeat for those who made you prey
    To parasite
    Appetites
Cannibals who swallowed you whole
Made carrion of body and soul

Is defiance to those who averted their eyes
    Drowned your cries
    In plausible lies
Then beat you down with sticks and stones
To bury their secrets with your bones

Is to see them shrivel hour by hour
    To watch them cower
    Before your power
Aged vipers, venom spent
Their evil insignificant

Is one more day between you and the past
    This will not last
    It's fading fast
Into the rear-view, distance-drowned
With every mile of hard-won ground

APPENDIX

You might be interested in knowing about the statue on the front cover. It was created by Dr. Michael Irving, a sculptor and a survivor of horrific child abuse himself. He is also a therapist (current title: well-being and quality of life coach), and Chris has been seeing him for years. If I was Chris's first godsend, Dr. Irving was definitely his second. But more about that in another book.

The statue we used for our cover is titled "Reaching Out." It is one of two figures designed for the Child Abuse Survivor Monument, a project Dr. Irving has been promoting for the past twenty years. He felt that, since there are memorials to soldiers and other heroes, the courageous people who are fighting their secret battles to survive child sexual abuse should be validated with a monument as well. It would also promote discussion of a subject that desperately needs more public consideration. Dr. Irving has been trying to find public space for his monument, approaching municipalities, universities, and other public bodies without success. He is currently discussing a site with a college north of Toronto.

The monument consists of two identical statues flanking a fountain. The most interesting feature of each statue is the pattern of quilt squares on its front and back. There over two hundred squares, each one designed by a survivor of childhood abuse. The square contains a cast of the person's hand, and words and other figures that express that person's struggle. There are blank squares included in the pattern: the monument is designed so viewers who wish to participate can dip their hands in the water, then leave their own handprints on a blank square. The inside of each statue also contains space for thousands of paper handprints, letters, poems, and other contributions from survivors all over North America and abroad.

If you want to know more about Dr. Irving and the Child Abuse Survivor Monument, you can go to www.childabusemonument.com. One remarkable facet of this website is the "Monument and Quilt Squares" feature, which allows you to click on any square on the statue's picture and see it up close. There is also the opportunity for survivors to send in handprints, etc., to be included on the monuments.

You have the opportunity to support the project, if you wish, by signing the petition to find the project a home. Dr. Irving's campaign would benefit from people demonstrating interest in the Child Abuse Survivor Monument, and it would be a wonderful way to get involved in supporting people like Chris.

ACKNOWLEDGEMENTS

This book was, on all counts, an unlikely accomplishment. I have never written a book before; nor did I ever plan to until I met Chris. I've *read* a lot of books — thousands, probably — so I know what a book is supposed to look like, but there is definitely more to it than that. I applied to the Humber School for Writers at Humber College in Toronto, and was accepted into the Creative Writing Program; they provided me with a writing coach, Karen "Kaz" Connelly, whose support and guidance got me through the hot mess of my rough draft.

Iguana Books, a publishing house in Toronto, took on my manuscript and wrestled it into publishable form. This was not fun; in addition to the usual difficulties, we had to deal with what I call the Gypsy Curse — the seriously weird run of bad luck that seemed to follow my efforts to help Chris, and now to get his story told. We lost the manuscript once, had to redo pages of notes that mysteriously disappeared, and kept getting emails blocked or spit back. Greg Ioannou, the president of Iguana Books, kept things together with the help of my project supervisor Meghan Behse. I had a whole team of editors, which felt pretty luxurious; Paula Chiarcos did the first full edit to smooth out the storyline, Toby Keymer caught gaffes and did general kvetching, and Heather Bury did the proofread.

Part of the difficulty, I'm sure, was my own ineptness with computers. I once beat a laptop to death because I couldn't reason with it, and I keep a supply of extra keyboards and mice for the times I get *really* frustrated. I contacted Seniors Tech Services, not because I am a senior (quite yet), but because I knew they must routinely deal with the kind of dumb questions I was going to be asking. My tutor, Vuso Moyana, has worked miracles in getting me to a level of minimal competence on the computer, and in troubleshooting many of the problems I was having transmitting and storing versions of the manuscript.

Finally, I'd like to thank my husband, Frank, for not divorcing me after I brought Chris into our home, and for eventually accepting him as part of the family. When two people marry, they become a third entity that can be stronger and better than either of them alone; and I don't think I could have been the person I needed to be in this situation without Frank.

www.ingramcontent.com/pod-product-compliance
Lightning Source LLC
Chambersburg PA
CBHW020527270326
41927CB00006B/471